"*When Religion Hurts You* is a wel~~~~
to leave the emotional terrain
and abuse. This book is an unde
guide toward not just 'treating'
journey toward healing. Anders~~~~   ...e reader
to their potential for addressing t.   _ ...ding in all the spaces
and places that lurk behind trauma. As she reminds us, *religious
trauma is trauma*."

—**Dr. Jennifer Mullan**, founder of Decolonizing Therapy, LLC

"*When Religion Hurts You* is a valuable addition to the robust literature on helping people recover from trauma due to either being born into a religious group that isn't healthy or being deceptively recruited into a religious cult. I am pleased to endorse this book and its recommendations."

—**Steven Hassan**, PhD, MEd, LMHC, NCC, founder
and director, Freedom of Mind Resource Center Inc.

"Laura Anderson's *When Religion Hurts You* is not simply about the ways high-demand religions can inflict pain on our bodies, souls, minds, and relationships—though it does explore this in insightful and concise ways. Anderson assures readers that beyond the hurt there is healing. Her approach deconstructs the notion that healing is something we can achieve one day in a rapture of beatific psychological bliss; rather, she reminds us that healing is a lifelong pilgrimage. Anderson offers two perspectives: one as a former insider, and one as a clinician who has spent decades focused on the ways religion hurts and the beauty of recovery, rediscovery, and renewal. Anderson's is a refreshing and hopeful voice during what feels for many of us like a time of great despair."

—**Bradley Onishi**, PhD, scholar and co-host of the *Straight
White American Jesus* podcast

"A brilliant blend of anecdotal and academic, this book offers a compassionate road map for those recovering from religious trauma. Dr. Anderson offers guidance on how to put lives back together and provides a thorough resource for mental health professionals to help them counsel others in the process. Poignant and personal, this book is a must-have for anyone in the muddy aftermath of their exit from high-control or extreme religious groups."

—Sarah Edmondson, author of *Scarred: The True Story of How I Escaped NXIVM, the Cult That Bound My Life*

"*When Religion Hurts You* is the most comprehensive, reflective, and helpful book about recovering from religious trauma and church abuse that I've ever read. Using research, personal experience, and her training as a therapist, Dr. Laura Anderson offers a powerful and poignant methodology toward healing. I needed to read *When Religion Hurts You*. Anderson's wisdom is practical and full of empathy, personal, and so very hopeful."

—Matthew Paul Turner, #1 *New York Times* bestselling author of *What Is God Like?*

"Dr. Laura Anderson has written a must-read for those who want to deconstruct the complexity of religious trauma through a lens that is not only scientific but also compassionate. This book is for every person who has experienced shame, guilt, self-doubt, and self-hate within religious contexts."

—Yolanda Renteria, licensed professional counselor

"Both compassionate and wise, *When Religion Hurts You* is the informative guide needed when making sense of and healing from the disorienting and painful experience of religious trauma. I plan to read and reread it, and I believe it will be a book people can come back to repeatedly on their path to individual and community healing."

—Hillary L. McBride, PhD, psychologist, author, speaker, podcaster

"When I first started drawing cartoons and writing posts about religious trauma, so many people claimed it was rare. Now we know differently, and more people are talking about it. I'm so thankful such a compassionate and wise professional like Dr. Laura Anderson has provided a valuable resource that will help people not only to understand what religious trauma is but also to find a holistic path of healing beyond it."

—David Hayward, a.k.a. NakedPastor

WHEN RELIGION
HURTS YOU

WHEN RELIGION HURTS YOU

Healing from Religious Trauma
and the Impact of High-Control Religion

LAURA E. ANDERSON, PhD

BrazosPress
a division of Baker Publishing Group
Grand Rapids, Michigan

Published by Brazos Press
a division of Baker Publishing Group
Grand Rapids, Michigan
www.brazospress.com

Printed in the United States of America

Library of Congress Cataloging-in-Publication Data
Names: Anderson, Laura E., 1982– author.
Title: When religion hurts you : healing from religious trauma and the impact of high-control religion / Laura E. Anderson, PhD.
Description: Grand Rapids, Michigan : Brazos Press, a division of Baker Publishing Group, 2023. | Includes bibliographical references.
Identifiers: LCCN 2023010858 | ISBN 9781587435881 (paperback) | ISBN 9781587436154 (casebound) | ISBN 9781493443154 (ebook) | ISBN 9781493443161 (pdf)
Subjects: LCSH: Psychological abuse victims—Religious life. | Psychological abuse victims—Rehabilitation. | Psychological abuse—Religious aspects—Christianity. | Religious addiction. | Christianity—Psychology.
Classification: LCC BV4596.P87 A54 2023 | DDC 204/.2—dc23/eng/20230701
LC record available at https://lccn.loc.gov/2023010858

Disclaimer: The names and details of the people and situations described in this book have been changed or presented in composite form to ensure the privacy of those with whom the author has worked.

Published in association with The Bindery Agency, www.TheBinderyAgency.com.

Baker Publishing Group publications use paper produced from sustainable forestry practices and post-consumer waste whenever possible.

23   24   25   26   27   28   29   7   6   5   4   3   2

For all who have been harmed by high-control religion,
who have suffered adverse religious experiences,
and who live with religious trauma.
May this book provide hope and healing—
abundant life does exist.

CONTENTS

ACKNOWLEDGMENTS

THERE ARE SO MANY PEOPLE who deserve mentioning and thanks for their instrumental role in inspiring this book and helping me bring it to life. I am so grateful for my clients and individuals I've met through social media and other public outlets, whose stories litter these pages and give so much hope. Thanks to the team at Brazos, especially my editor, Katelyn, for giving me the opportunity to write this book. My agent, Trinity, believed not only that this book should be written but that I should be the one to write it.

To my family: despite our differences, I am grateful that you love me and support me.

To Tia: I am so grateful for your friendship and for the support you have provided me in this process, for talking through things, offering feedback, encouraging me, keeping me grounded, challenging me, and offering your hope and certainty that this book could be what it is until I realized it for myself.

To my friends: each of you has inspired me, challenged me, given me hope, kept me going, laughed with me, cried with me, and shown me that healing from trauma is worth it because it means I can be in relationship with you! So to Adam and Heather, Elizabeth and Jason, Kristen, Rachel and Justin, Sara, Shay, Kevin, Blair,

Wade and Patrick, Jessica, Jeremy, Travis and Lonnie, David and Karina, Kenna, Kelli, Drew, Andrew, Jon, Lindsay, Seerut, Doug, Jack, Zach, and Jen: I love you all!

To the practitioners at the Center for Trauma Resolution and Recovery and Brian Peck, Kendra Snyder, and Kayla Felten, our conversations, dreaming, brainstorming, and passion for those who have experienced harm from religion have helped me grow as a professional and as a human; I love being able to work alongside each one of you!

To Phoebe: thanks for being my best friend and the little creature who demonstrates unconditional love even on my edgiest of days.

ABBREVIATIONS

ACE	adverse childhood experience
ACES	Adverse Childhood Experiences Study
ANS	autonomic nervous system
ARE	adverse religious experience
CPTSD	complex post-traumatic stress disorder
DID-NOS	dissociative identity disorder, not otherwise specified
EMDR	eye movement desensitization and reprocessing
HCR	high-control religion
OCD	obsessive-compulsive disorder
PFC	prefrontal cortex
PNS	parasympathetic nervous system
PTSD	post-traumatic stress disorder
RTI	Religious Trauma Institute
SES	social engagement system
SNS	sympathetic nervous system

Introduction

IN THE SOUTH, when you meet someone new, the question after asking their name is "Where do you go to church?" Nashville, where I live, is home to many religious and conservative organizations, including large churches, colleges and universities, and the Southern Baptist Convention headquarters.

When I opened my therapy practice, I understood that spiritual abuse happened far more often than most people let on. People regularly sat on my couch and told me about deeply painful experiences they had endured from their pastors, ministry leaders, family, and friends, all in the name of God.

As the US presidential election of 2016 drew near, more and more of my clients expressed disillusionment at what they were seeing. Bewildered, they described the hurt and betrayal they felt as friends, family, and people they looked up to as their spiritual authorities enthusiastically supported a presidential candidate who for all intents and purposes seemed to be the antithesis of Christlike—at least according to what they had been taught their whole lives. Despite these supporters calling Donald Trump "God's

---

All the stories shared in this book are true, but many are composites that convey the magnitude and impact of what happened while protecting the identities of those involved. All names and identifying information have been changed.

man," my disillusioned clients lamented that he was nothing like the Jesus they had given up everything to follow.

The day after Trump was elected president, the energy in my office was thick and heavy. Clients sat in tears, feeling confused and betrayed by the people they had trusted most. The questions they had been tentatively asking about life, faith, and God took on new vigor as they grieved the lives they once knew. They began realizing they needed to embark on a journey to understand and untangle what they had been told to be true and to find a new foundation to stand on. On top of this, many of my clients reported physiological and psychological symptoms consistent with trauma, extreme stress, and shame, all of which mere cognitive shifting couldn't help.

I had extensive knowledge of trauma myself by this point—due both to my personal experiences and my professional work and education. Some of their triggers and responses were reflective of post-traumatic stress disorder (PTSD); others exhibited complex trauma from enduring decades of religious indoctrination and practices in their family of origin and churches. As clients relayed their experiences (many of them allowing themselves permission to be accurate and honest for the first time in their lives), we discovered dynamics of systemic power and control, religious and spiritual abuse, harm, and other adverse experiences that now, outside of the religious environment, were able to be seen for what they truly were and in many cases resulted in what felt like life falling apart.

WHILE THE FIRST FOUR CHAPTERS of this book will focus on what trauma is and how it functions in and must be healed through the body, for now it is essential to recognize this: *religious trauma is trauma.*

Once clients and colleagues alike caught wind that I was interested and versed in religious trauma and abuse, my practice quickly filled up. As an entrepreneur, this was an excellent problem to have, but as a clinician who deeply desired to help others, I knew I needed to be innovative in finding ways to do this work.

In January 2019, I began my practicum for my PhD. I pitched to my professor that I could use this time to create a resource for other mental health professionals that would educate them on religious trauma, abuse, and adverse religious experiences (AREs). My project was accepted, and I went straight to Twitter to ask my meager following a simple question: *What do you wish your therapist knew about religious trauma?*

Being new to social media, I figured I would get a handful of responses. Hundreds came through in a couple days. I knew I was on the right track as so many people expressed both gratitude that this resource was being created and frustration that they so often had to educate their therapist—or worse, *convince* their therapist—that religious trauma was real. I was also able to connect with a handful of mental health professionals who found themselves in the same spot as me: desperately needing other qualified professionals to refer an overwhelming number of clients to.

Through these interactions, I cofounded the Religious Trauma Institute (RTI). I also cocreated the concept of AREs (which we will examine further in chap. 3). My RTI cofounder, Brian Peck, and I teamed up with the founders of the Reclamation Collective (a nonprofit organization offering support to religious trauma survivors) to create a trauma-informed foundation for understanding religious trauma. To our knowledge, we were some of the first therapists working with religious trauma who were *not* antireligious and who approached religious trauma and healing from religious trauma using up-to-date trauma research. Our priorities included educating other mental health professionals and healers, supporting survivors through resolving trauma in the body, recovering from the unique harm religion can inflict individually and collectively, and reclaiming one's life as a healing individual.

Limitations around Healing

Decades of participating in high-control religion combined with relational and sexualized violence left me with wounds and scars that, in spite of my attempts to heal, remained open and raw. I was dismayed that I was still experiencing physiological and psychological symptoms from earlier life experiences; I often felt helpless. I thought healing had a very specific look: physically, relationally, socially, emotionally, and spiritually. But despite my years of diligent therapy work, healing seemed further away than ever before.

Despite declaring that I would never go back to school, I decided to pursue a PhD in mind-body medicine. I vowed not only to be healed by the end of my program but also to somehow include my healing process in my doctoral research as I completed my dissertation.

But just a couple months into the program, while taking a somatic (relating to the body) therapy course, my hopes of being healed came crashing down. It was as if my body woke up from a deep slumber, and suddenly *everything* seemed to get worse. Due to this, the focus of my healing and research began to shift. While I could not deny that many of my symptoms had intensified, there were other areas where I was getting better. I struggled to understand how these two things could be happening at once.

In a meeting with my dissertation chair, she gently urged me to sit with the concept of healing as I understood it and notice if there were any limitations around it. I began to ponder my definition of what it meant to be "healed from trauma." Since I knew I would be using my journals as a source of data for my research, I began to flip through the pages chronicling decades of my life. I noticed different patterns and themes. Where I had previously seen an unresolved issue, I now noticed that I had gained more insight each time I circled back to the issue. As I read my descriptions of what was happening in my life at a given moment, I could

4

remember what it felt like to be in my body at those times—and I could easily recognize that I no longer felt that way. Other times I could see that there were places I still felt stuck, but how I viewed them now was different.

I noticed that each time I wrote about not being healed in the way I wanted, I was missing the healing *that was happening right in front of me.* My definition of what healing looked like was making it nearly impossible to see the ways that I had grown, changed, and experienced healing.

Tentatively—as if I were trying something on for size—I began to wonder if my definition of healing was *limiting* the process. I wondered if being healed was not a fixed point that I would arrive at one day, where I could put a period at the end of a sentence and say, "There! I am done healing." Instead, I wondered if healing could be an ongoing and dynamic process that was multidimensional and included small moments of change and awareness.

Redefining Healing

Initially, I felt terrified to let go of the idea that I had created as the prize at the finish line. I lamented that I might have to live with some of the impacts of trauma for the remainder of my life. This felt unfair. (Truthfully, it *still* feels unfair!) But shifting my definition of healing opened space for other options and possibilities. Redefining healing as an ongoing process and not an end point allowed room for every tiny moment in the day when I tuned in to my body, felt something, responded differently, or engaged with self-awareness, to be seen as progress.

It struck me that my original conception of healing—that unless I arrived at a specific destination I was not healed—was flawed. It wasn't lost on me that this was like the religious system in which I had grown up. I was taught to live my life with a specific end goal in mind: heaven. Anything else didn't matter.

The idea of healing being ongoing, like sanctification, felt heavy. It seemed like the messages I was trying to discard—suffering happens for a reason; all things work together for good; God doesn't give us more than we can handle—were haunting me again. I struggled with the idea that my former religion was correct about suffering and pain. I later came to recognize that sanctification and healing have two distinctly different motivations. Sanctification *does* have an end goal: heaven. And with that, sanctification dismisses walking through pain and instead focuses on the point of growth or on finding a reason for the pain. Healing, however, is motivated by life on this earth—moving through the pain because healing ourselves allows us to live full and vibrant lives for ourselves, in relation to others and the world. Healing is not about circumventing pain or even being pain-free but about walking *through* the pain and trauma so that they don't define us, thereby allowing for depth, compassion, kindness, and empathy toward ourselves and others. For me, it didn't take long before healing sounded nothing like sanctification.

Redefining healing as an ongoing process became like a pair of glasses that helped me see more clearly. Many experiences that I had previously written off I could now see were clearly moments of healing, but I had downplayed their significance because it wasn't *the* end goal I had in mind. But by wearing the new glasses of healing as a lifelong process, I could see that I *was* healing. I was feeling emotions and developing self-awareness, I had begun a relationship with my body, I wasn't scared all the time, my anxiety and depression were significantly decreasing, people didn't feel as threatening, and so much more.

As I deconstructed my faith, and learned later in my research on healing, I realized that when the end goal is already set, we often miss everything else that's happening. When my focus was on eternity in heaven and the specific ways that I needed to live to get there, I missed life on earth. I was so concerned with living, eating, drinking, dressing, behaving, worshiping, relating, thinking, and feeling exactly as had been prescribed, that days, weeks, and even years went by when I had no idea what had actually happened. Similarly, when I fixated on the end goal of being healed, I designed my life to achieve that ideal and subsequently missed everything else that was happening in my life—including the ways I was suffering and creating more pain for myself by trying to achieve a goal that felt out of reach.

I began scouring academic library databases for research on healing. I found ample research on trauma, symptoms of trauma, healing trauma, and even a concept called post-traumatic growth, but I found almost no research about ongoing healing after trauma. Most research defined healing as either symptom alleviation or symptom reduction, but this felt oversimplified and seemed to reduce the multidimensional way that trauma impacts individuals. No wonder my idea of healing was defined as a static end point; the data were *also* focused on this definition.

I began shifting in my own clinical practice—immediately. While many of my clients were seeing significant reduction and alleviation of their symptoms and even felt like they were creating a new life for themselves, they also were discouraged when they felt triggered, didn't stick to a boundary, felt angry, or struggled to make new friends. Clients often felt overwhelmed when their experience of a trigger and the subsequent physiological response seemed to signal that they weren't healed. They thought they needed to start over.

Though they were hesitant to accept a new definition of healing and often agonized over the thought of healing as a lifelong process, they also began to notice that shifting to this definition opened a new world to them. They experienced less shame. They realized that their experiences were momentary and didn't have eternal significance. They could celebrate each moment—small or large—when they did something different, even if they didn't get the results they thought they should.

Though the focus on healing as an ongoing and dynamic process didn't resolve the trauma they experienced, it did allow healing to take on a more nuanced definition. This increased their feelings of hopefulness and empowerment, and it helped them recognize the inherent goodness they possessed within them—often for the first time.

What This Book Is About

This book is a culmination of my doctoral research, clinical experience, and personal story. While I won't be laying out a step-by-step process of how to heal trauma or guaranteeing specific outcomes, I want to inspire hope that living in a healing body is possible after experiencing religious trauma.

In chapter 1, I tell my story of living within a high-control religion (HCR). My hope is that my experience may provide a sense of connection and togetherness for those reading this book. My interest in working with religious trauma survivors professionally stems from my own experiences and the journey of healing that I am living.

In chapters 2–4, I provide an overview of what trauma is and discuss religious abuse, AREs, and the nervous system. I am an eclectic practitioner and human, which means that I do not suggest one "right" way to do healing work. Each person is unique, and their experiences are subjective. What works for me in my own healing journey may or may not be helpful for you. This book does not take the place of therapy or any other healing practice that is meaningful to you. I am merely looking at the research to offer a better understanding of what religious trauma is so that you can make choices regarding your own trauma resolution and recovery.

Chapters 5–13 outline nine key areas that are impacted when one embarks on a healing journey, based on my doctoral research, clinical experiences, and personal story. It's important to note that this list is not exhaustive; healing can manifest in a life in many other ways. Some of the chapters may resonate more strongly with you than others. Each chapter will discuss how HCR influenced the specific theme as well as how someone may experience living in a healing body after religious trauma.

THE METHODOLOGY OF RESEARCH I used for my doctoral dissertation was autopsychography, which means that my life and experiences were the motivation and foundation for this research. This may mean that my findings feel incomplete or reductive to you, since they don't consider your unique experiences and the complexities of who you are as a person. Though I tried to incorporate others' stories and experiences, I want to acknowledge that the intersections of who I am affect how I've experienced healing, my access to resources, and the ease or difficulty with which I've moved through the healing process. From an academic standpoint, this demonstrates why it is so important to do more research on the markers of living in a healing body after trauma—so that diverse voices and experiences are heard, considered, and valued.

I felt emotional when I presented my oral defense of my doctoral research to my committee—the people who would determine whether I had completed all the necessary requirements to become Dr. Laura Anderson. I felt nervous and anxious (this was, after all, the culmination of years of academic work). But there was another feeling I couldn't quite put my finger on—an awareness that I was about to do something big, that my research was important, and that my work was honoring the journey I had been on.

My presentation was flawless, thanks to many hours of practice, and when I turned to look at my committee after sharing my closing thoughts, I saw tears streaming down their faces. We sat in silence. The moment felt sacred. I realized that what I had been feeling leading up to the presentation was the feeling of holiness. Not the holiness of formal religion but a sense of awe, connectedness, and hope. It was an experience I will never forget.

I don't think things happen to us for a reason. I don't think there is some all-knowing force directing our lives so that we can learn a lesson and pass on that knowledge to others. I don't think I had to go through what I did to get this book into your hands. In fact, there were many other ways I could have learned those lessons—and they could have been learned without excruciating pain. Yet I cannot deny that somehow my experiences also turned me into who I am and resulted in this book being in your hands today. Multiple things can be true at the same time.

Regardless of the hows and the whys, I feel honored to be able to share with you this research, anecdotes from others, and parts of my own story, so that perhaps you too can be inspired to keep going on this healing journey—while also celebrating how far you have already come.

1

My Story

WHEN I WAS A SMALL CHILD, I lay in bed every night imagining Jesus dying on the cross. It was a story I had been told from the moment I was born: I was a sinner and Jesus died for me so that I could go to heaven and spend eternity with him. If I didn't accept what he had done, I would have to spend eternity in hell. At younger than five years old, there was no way I could cognitively understand what I was being taught. All I knew is that I needed to figure out a way to get to heaven. The phrase "accepting Jesus into your heart" was one I heard from the mouths of pastors, Sunday school teachers, and my parents, but no one was clear on how to do that. So every night for years I imagined Jesus, nailed to the cross, dying for my sins. It was my way of hoping that if Jesus came back while I was sleeping, he would have favor on me.

On the first day of kindergarten, I convinced my mom that I needed to ask Jesus into my heart. I'm not sure what it was that made the first day of kindergarten *the* day where I possessed more understanding than days in the past. Nevertheless, on that day she sat with me at the kitchen table and said the words, which I repeated back, that meant that I had gained security into heaven. Later that evening we celebrated. My parents referred to that day as my spiritual birthday, and every year for decades I received gifts, cards, or calls from them, reminding me of the day I made the most important decision of my life.

Though I cannot say that this day marked any profound shift inside me, it officially marked my spiritual journey. Despite there never having been a time when I wasn't attending a church, participating in extra church activities, or hearing the Bible being read to me at home, asking Jesus into my heart to be the savior of my life was the day that, at five years old, I committed the rest of my life to following God.

Several years later, my parents informed my siblings and me that we would be moving to a rural area in Minnesota because God had called us to work at a church camp. Our family had gone there a few times and spent our weeks riding horses, swimming at the lake, and building campfires. What kid wouldn't love this? But I was apprehensive. Everything about our life would change: we would be a ministry family and unbeknownst to me and my siblings at the time, living at a camp wasn't all fun and games . . . literally. While the summer was filled with kids and weekends were filled with retreats, we lived quite a distance from our school, church, friends, and family. During the summers we lived in a world where crazy games, fast-paced activities, and chapel services were our normal. It was easy to forget there was a world outside. Every summer until my junior year of high school, I didn't see any of my friends from school for three months because of camp.

Camp life was unconcerned with school friends, relationship drama, the latest fads, or being popular. Instead we were focused on living for Christ, being on fire for God, and making commitments for abstinence and sexual purity so that we could be different from our peers. Not shockingly, my friends at school didn't understand my camp bubble and were uninterested in hearing about the things that were important in the camp bubble.

During my middle school years, a campaign swept the nation: True Love Waits. It was the first thing that bridged my God-world and my school-world. Since I went to school a significant distance from the church I attended, I often kept these two worlds apart. But when the campaign came to rural Minnesota, teenagers at both school and church were excited about it. I was a late bloomer when it came to puberty and adolescence. While I was interested in boys and had my share of crushes, I was terrified to act on them because I believed them to be a sin. Experiences from early childhood such as my crush on the neighbor boy and asking a boy, when I was in third grade, if he liked me were not received well by my parents. I took this to mean that, at the very least, liking a boy was not honoring my father and mother, and I *knew* that was a sin.

When the church youth pastor began talking to us about abstinence, virginity, and sex, I nodded along as if I understood. We were told about God's plans for sex and that anything outside that plan was not only a sin but evidence that perhaps we were not Christians at all. The decision to sign the True Love Waits pledge card was not a difficult one. I signed my name, was applauded by the congregation, and, a few years later, received a purity ring from my parents.

The True Love Waits campaign crossed the divide between religious and secular cultures through its marketing. Though some celebrities shared publicly about their own abstinence commitments and though abstinence-only sex education was nationally funded in schools, I still didn't understand the commitment I had made. Intuitively, however, I recognized the biological changes happening in my body to be a source of shame and disgust. Though I desperately wanted a boyfriend, I quickly became repulsed if someone liked me back because I feared it meant my body had caused them to lust. While I know now that I had hormones raging through my body, back then the sensations and shifts inside me felt scary and foreign. My junior year of high school, Dannah Gresh's book *And the Bride Wore White* was published as a comprehensive guide on how to live a pure lifestyle—one that would lead toward my life purpose: to be married and have children. For years I used that book as a guide to and foundation for how I should live; I was floundering, and purity culture (though not called that then) felt like a stable foundation I could stand on.

By my senior year I was perplexed about what I should do next. I had academic, artistic, and musical credentials that would allow for my choice in schools, and I received an acceptance letter and an appealing financial aid package from each college I applied to. I was confused though because I had no idea what I wanted to do with my life. On the one hand, I knew the world was bigger than what I had been shown; on the other hand, the pinnacle of my life was to be a wife and mother, and I didn't need a degree or the student debt that came with it to fulfill that role. As I watched my closest friends excitedly go off to colleges, I resigned myself to trying to make the best out of community college.

As I walked out of my high school graduation ceremony, a weight descended on me. I realized that every decision from this point forward would impact the rest of my life. While this statement is true for adults in general, the weight of this decision felt even more intense because my Reformed theology taught me that finding God's plan for my life was a little bit like finding a needle in a haystack. Every choice I made had an eternal consequence. Perhaps when I chose my shirt in the morning before I went to my classes, I chose the wrong shirt, one that would be off-putting to a man who passed by me who was supposed to be my future husband. Instead of seeing my wise and godly character, he would be repulsed by my shirt choice, and my chances at marriage and children would be dashed. Though at the time I was unaware of mental health diagnoses, I know now that I developed severe anxiety and religious scrupulosity (a form of religious obsessive-compulsive disorder), and eventually depression, that no amount of Bible reading, prayer, repentance, or discipleship seemed to lift.

Experiences of Religious Abuse

At church one Sunday after I graduated, the youth pastor, Tray, approached me. My stomach began to churn because I intuited that he was about to ask me to volunteer to work with the middle school youth group. Being a youth leader sounded like the worst possible way to spend my time. But when he told me that God had revealed to him that I would be an excellent small group leader, who was I to argue with him? Or God? Masking my frustration, I agreed to attend the youth leader retreat a few weeks later.

I did like the youth staff and was enamored with Tray. He had a magnetic presence—and more than that, he took an interest in me. He complimented what he called my raw talent and skills, bragged about me in front of other leaders, and would glance at me when he told jokes, as if he wanted to make sure I laughed. I found myself getting more involved in the youth group because I enjoyed that attention. Months into the first year of volunteering with the youth group, Tray asked me if I would help lead an upcoming mission trip. I couldn't understand why we should go to different locales to minister to people when we had enough people in our own community who needed the same gospel, but I understood that such questions would not be well received. However, when Tray asked me to be the main teacher, I accepted without hesitation. Months after that, when his ministry assistant decided to quit, he hired me to take her spot. At barely nineteen years old, I was in a prime position of serving God; I was visible to a godly man, and I was creating the life I had been told was for me.

Tray and I became a dynamic team; he showered me with compliments, gave me special attention, shared his innermost thoughts and secrets, and told me how lucky he was to have me working for him. I became friends with his wife and babysat his children, often spending many nights a week at their house, staying up late to talk and dream about ministry. Despite initially being hired for an assistant role, I accepted projects and tasks that went far beyond my pay grade because Tray said he saw potential in me and promised that if I could prove my capability in these roles, then I could be considered for other, more prestigious positions. Eventually, I became the person that people had to go through to access him. He said he trusted me and valued my opinions and that he was willing to listen only to people in his inner circle—which I was.

Though my parents were members of the church, Tray confided in me that I needed someone who was further along spiritually, like he was, to guide me. I welcomed the invitation to look to him as a spiritual authority, and his words became a source of unquestionable truth. When he told me he knew me better than I knew myself, I believed him. When he told me I was special, I was over the moon. When he told me there was nothing really special about me, I was devastated and ashamed, but I believed him then too.

The first instance of overt spiritual abuse I experienced, though I was unable to categorize it as that at the time, came shortly after I began working at the church, when the senior high youth pastor, Phillip, ventured into the office I shared with his assistant, fuming. He ranted at me as his assistant looked on. He accused me of doing a task incorrectly and then lying about it. Baffled, I tried to defend myself, knowing that the task in question was his assistant's responsibility. Eventually he was yelling at me—to the point where an assistant from another department came into our office suite to close the door. Before leaving my office, Phillip warned me to not speak of what happened to anyone, noting that if I did, I would be sinning since he was my spiritual authority.

Despite this harsh warning, I simply could not hold in what had happened to me. I recognized that something was wrong but was dismayed when I later told Tray what happened only to have him affirm what Phillip had told me. Believing that the only choice I had was to apologize or risk losing my job, I chose the former and made my way to Phillip's office to ask for forgiveness.

By the early 2000s, many books had been written about various topics within purity culture: how to have a godly relationship, physical intimacy, boundaries, modesty, roles for men and women, purity of heart and mind, and everything in between. I devoured the books looking for any small or large characteristic or action I could change that would make me appealing to a man. I assumed that my singleness was both the result of some hidden sin I hadn't repented of as well as God trying to teach me a lesson. When I was brave enough to share my frustrations about being single, I was often told that I wanted marriage too much and that God wouldn't give me a husband until I was satisfied in him. Or that I needed to use this season of singleness to learn how to submit and to seek mentorship from older women in the church.

By this point I had learned that I needed to trust others' voices and direction for me. To keep me accountable, I also mentored girls in the youth group outside of my small group and created purity culture curriculum so that I could train the younger girls to become godly wives and mothers. I vowed to not kiss prior to my wedding day and learned to suppress all sexual desires—so much so that I wondered if I was asexual. Despite my absolute fascination with sex and relationships, I could explore this fascination only through the hatred of them in an effort to do things the godly way.

A few years into my position at the church, I was still single, and a mutual interest developed between one of the other leaders and me. Unfortunately, Lucas was four years my junior and finishing his senior year of high school. We decided that nothing could happen between us until he graduated a couple months later. Since we were both committed to living a life of purity in body, heart, and mind, I informed Tray of my interest in Lucas. He was enraged and threatened harsh consequences if I acted on my interest.

When Lucas graduated from high school, Tray informed other church leaders of my plans to allow Lucas to pursue a relationship with me, and they decided that I was not permitted to have a relationship with him. Despite my compliance, Tray became furious with me for even entertaining a relationship that was not sanctioned by him and encouraged others to report back to him anytime I was seen in public. I was regularly accused of things I had not done and was unable to defend myself since Tray had already determined I was living in sin. Routinely, I was stripped of tasks in my paid and volunteer work and was told I wasn't allowed any youth group student contact and that I wasn't fit to shepherd other leaders. My work was eventually reduced to administrative tasks. After several months of this, I told Tray I would quit. He responded that he was relieved because if I hadn't, he would have fired me for failure to submit to spiritual authority.

The public reason for my departure from my position at the church was that I was going to move so I could go back to school, which was true. I began applying for master's programs and jobs a few hours away, and I fully intended to move. Initially the process of applying for schools and jobs was easy; I had many promising opportunities to choose from. One by one, however, I received calls and letters indicating that I would no longer be a fit for the program or job I had applied for. I later learned that people at the church had contacted the places I was interested in to warn them about me.

Beginning to Deconstruct

Eventually I took a job at a local community college and began a process of repentance and restoration with church leadership. The community college was the first environment I worked in that was not tied to ministry or God. I was shocked by the respect I received for the work that I did and by the fact that my being a woman didn't hinder me. Though I did not particularly enjoy working at the college, it allowed me to see that I could pursue additional education and even move away. So without telling anyone, I began the application process again to attend graduate school and a couple years later, I quietly made plans to move.

I attended Liberty University for my master's degree program. Though the school has received much negative press, I look back on my time in Liberty's hybrid master's degree program with relative fondness. Their education was good, and I felt prepared to enter the field of therapy. Simultaneously, the leadership at the church changed, which allowed me to work my way back into its protective covering. Despite knowing I wanted to move, I thought that being outside the protection of the church meant that the devil could get ahold of me, which was terrifying, so I used every opportunity to prove my usefulness.

Eventually I, along with three others, started a large young adult ministry in the community, and I was given all administrative and event-planning tasks, on top of teaching leadership courses, mentoring, and being expected to be available at any moment. Despite being a full-time student with an unpaid internship, I was asked to give more time and other resources to the ministry and to support the pastor and his wife leading the ministry. I eventually quit both of my meager paying jobs so that I could focus more of my time on ministry. Between my volunteer work and schoolwork, most of my hours were filled. Though student loans covered most of my expenses, I still needed to pick up as many side jobs as I could to make ends meet.

By the time I graduated from Liberty, I was so burned out that moving away from everything familiar felt like a relief. Knowing that I now had a career that would make it easier to support myself, I jumped at the first opportunity I was given to move. I never looked back. Starting over with a new life seemed less scary than spending one more day in the life I had been living.

I moved to Nashville and started attending a church that, while billing itself as progressive, still preached the same messages I grew up with. Though the process of my religious deconstruction and deconversion will be detailed, in part, later in this book, for now what's important to know is that the church did offer me a place to ask questions. I experienced immense relief in simply being allowed to voice my uncertainties without my salvation being called into question. It was at this church that I would eventually meet a now-former partner with whom I would continue my deconstruction process, reevaluate my purity culture commitments, and ultimately leave the church. Despite the relationship being characterized by dynamics of power and control, domestic violence, and abuse—adding to the religious trauma that I already was suffering from—I can still maintain a sense of fondness toward a time in that relationship where I was able to try out life apart from the fundamentalist patterns of living that had been the entirety of my existence. Ultimately, processing this relationship in therapy opened my eyes to the spiritual abuse, harm, and AREs that I had undergone.

I went through a long journey to understand that the way my body responded to the HCR I was a part of resulted in trauma. My deconstruction journey began over a decade before I recognized that I had been traumatized. Trauma has traditionally been understood as the event that happened. It wasn't until I began having panic attacks, flashbacks, and visceral somatic symptoms on the one-year anniversary of leaving a physically and psychologically harmful job that a therapist gently introduced me to eye movement desensitization and reprocessing (EMDR) therapy—the most well-known trauma therapy modality at the time. Though neither of us discussed the possibility of trauma as it pertained to the panic and flashbacks around my previous job, EMDR was incredibly helpful in my therapy. At a certain point, however, while the intensity of the work experiences had decreased and were no longer scary, I was still experiencing symptoms in my body, having flashbacks to earlier events in my life, and feeling a constant sense of dread, panic, and anxiety.

Though my therapist genuinely wanted to help, my body seemed resistant, and I began to dissociate and was unable to tolerate EMDR whenever we tried to discuss any overwhelming events outside of my job.[1] I eventually quit therapy because it felt like a waste of time and my symptoms were getting worse. By this point I was quite isolated and had significant social anxiety. I was experiencing extreme weight gain, increased depression and anxiety, insomnia, inability to concentrate, near-constant dissociation, digestive issues, exhaustion, and hypervigilance. Though I had cut out most of the people, places, and things in my life that were causing distress, the experience of living in my body every day was getting more difficult.

Eventually things were so bad that dissociation was the safest way to live; though I was physically present, I was mentally absent. Many times I ended up somewhere in or around my house with no recollection of getting there. I would often sit on the couch for what I thought was ten minutes only to discover that hours had gone by. Emotions escaped me, laughing was impossible, anywhere other than work or my house felt scary, and I only felt safe spending time with three individuals. I required rigid boundaries because life felt scary and intolerable.

Despite a growing list of symptoms, I couldn't get answers from medical or mental health professionals. Doctors were stumped when my external appearance indicated hypothyroidism, but my blood tests indicated near *hyper*thyroidism. Specialists couldn't understand how all their recommendations for sleep still resulted in extreme exhaustion and insomnia. Still, no one mentioned trauma. To be fair, I didn't recognize the symptoms as trauma either.

Several years later, my therapist casually dropped the term "complex post-traumatic stress disorder" (CPTSD) in conversation,

1. Trauma research suggests that when an individual undergoes extreme stress and overwhelming and/or prolonged traumatic experiences, as is often the case with religious trauma, individuals learn how to dissociate—that is, to mentally leave their bodies to protect themselves from a real or perceived threat. See Judith Herman, *Trauma and Recovery: The Aftermath of Violence—From Domestic Abuse to Political Terror* (New York: Basic Books, 1992).

assuming that I already knew this was my diagnosis. I stared back at her blankly, and she paused to educate me on CPTSD. Immediately I knew this diagnosis fit with what I was experiencing, which brought me significant relief because I knew that I was not making my symptoms and distress up in my head, that what I was experiencing was real, and that, yes, it really was *that bad*.

Why Share My Story

I'm often asked why I have made a career out of working with individuals who have had AREs or experienced faith deconstruction, purity culture, religious trauma, and the like. Truly, my passion for working with them and my extensive research and training in trauma is motivated by my own experiences. What you've read above is just the tip of the iceberg regarding my own story. I contemplated giving more details and sharing more experiences, but I am more interested in the process of healing than in what I have experienced.

We live in a voyeuristic culture where salacious stories are regularly shared—almost expected—to prove that what we went through was that bad. We often use this as a way to compare trauma—that is, to see who had it worse. This almost always breeds shame. While our stories are important, my story does not need to provide a baseline or act as a measuring stick that determines if how you experienced and were impacted by an HCR is valid. It is valid. Because you experienced it.

As I will discuss in this book, trauma is not the event or the thing that happened to us; rather, it is the way our bodies and nervous systems respond to what happened to us. Operating from this premise allows us to consider that since religious trauma does not stem from specific practices, doctrines, or beliefs, this book could be for anyone—regardless of the sect, denomination, or group we belong or belonged to. My experience comes from a strict fundamentalist, evangelical, Reformed theological background, and my stories reflect that lived experience. While I cannot speak to the lived experiences of someone who belonged to Mormon, Muslim, Jehovah's Witness, Catholic, or other churches and denominations, my research and training allow me to understand how trauma may live in that person's body the same way that it lived in mine. This means that even if you do not share my background, this book may still help you understand how religious trauma is trauma and how to reclaim your life.

Finally, it's important to me to recognize and own that I was once someone who participated in harming others through religious practices, rules, beliefs, and doctrine. I was someone who was in a position of spiritual authority, and I used my position and influence in ways that I now know caused people harm. In some cases, I have been able to talk to, apologize to, and repair relationships with some of the people I hurt, but I know there are many more people out there.

While it is true that I was doing what was done to and modeled for me, I also recognize that I must own the choices I made as an adult who was in relationship with others and in a position of influence. I taught harmful doctrine; I shamed people into behavioral change; I reported back to church leadership about specific people; I was judgmental, cold, unrelenting, and manipulative. I spread messages that promoted patriarchy, ableism, misogyny, capitalism, and racism. I know that there are people who were and are in pain because of how I acted and interacted in my ministry days. For this, I am deeply apologetic and regretful.

I recognize that there may be people who struggle to believe or accept my apology, and I can both understand and respect that. To them I would say this: your acceptance of my apology or forgiveness of my actions in no way determines your healing. Forgiveness is not a precursor for being truly healed; forgiveness doesn't need to be part of healing at all. Your story and experiences matter, and I truly do hope that you are able to live as a healing individual.

2

What Is Religious Trauma?

THE QUESTION I AM ASKED MOST FREQUENTLY IS "What is religious trauma?" To understand religious trauma, we must first understand what trauma is. Up until the past few decades, trauma was thought of primarily as something that happens *to* you—a thing or an event such as what soldiers experience in war. The term "trauma" evolved from the earlier condition called "shell shock," which became accepted colloquially during World War I but was likely used long before that, as far back as the Civil War. We now categorize shell shock as post-traumatic stress disorder (PTSD), but it was originally thought to be the result of soldiers being exposed to exploding shells. Soldiers often experienced symptoms such as helplessness, panic, or an inability to reason, sleep, walk, or talk.

Trauma researcher Bessel van der Kolk began his clinical work with veterans of the Vietnam War. Eager to provide them with relief, he used the common therapeutic interventions of the time, most notably a technique called "in vivo" or "gradual exposure," where the client is slowly subjected to the scary event or trigger with the goal of desensitization.[1] At that time, treatment was considered successful if an individual's symptoms were reduced. By 1980, the American Psychological Association changed the term "shell shock" to PTSD and defined it as a catastrophic stressor that was outside the range of normal human experience. Occurrences such as natural disasters, rape, war, car accidents, torture, and other abnormal stressors were thought to be significant enough to cause long-term symptoms that impeded one's ability to live a normal life.

Though the setting aside of the term "shell shock" and the inclusion of PTSD in one of the foremost diagnostic manuals was a significant step in validating trauma survivors and allowing access to care, researchers like van der Kolk noticed the shortcomings of the diagnosis. He recognized that the physiological symptoms his clients were experiencing were not entirely alleviated by gradual exposure therapy or by shifting their thoughts. Moreover, many individuals who had never gone to war or experienced catastrophic events were experiencing symptoms of trauma.

Complex Trauma

In 1992, researcher and educator Judith Herman presented her groundbreaking research that trauma is *not* limited to catastrophic events. Rather, trauma is the result of the physiological experience of overwhelm—which happens when something that is too much, too fast, or too soon threatens our ability to cope and return to a felt sense of safety and could be set off by virtually anything. Herman's research expands the definition of PTSD to include a more complex version of it, ultimately resulting in the diagnosis we know today as complex PTSD or CPTSD. Herman indicates that CPTSD is the result of prolonged and repeated experiences

1. Bessel van der Kolk, *The Body Keeps the Score: Brain, Mind, and Body in the Healing of Trauma* (New York: Penguin Books, 2015).

of overwhelm that are characteristic in situations such as childhood abuse, domestic violence, repeated sexual exploitation, situations of coercive control, and religious cults. Herman suggests that many of these experiences include the concept of being held captive to some degree.[2]

Herman's proposal of the CPTSD diagnosis includes three main differences from what had been formally accepted as PTSD at that point. The first difference relates to the individual's symptoms: CPTSD survivors have symptoms that are often more complex and all-encompassing than those of PTSD survivors. The second difference is the character of the individual with CPTSD, who often develops personality changes that impair and impact their identity and how they relate to others. The third difference is survivors' vulnerability to instances or cycles of repeated harm, both self-inflicted and at the hands of others.

Herman was joined by other pioneers such as van der Kolk, Peter Levine (developer of the Somatic Experiencing Trauma-Resolution Model), and Stephen Porges (creator of the polyvagal theory). These researchers found that trauma is a subjective, perceptive, and physiological response to a person, place, or thing that overwhelms the nervous system's natural capacity to cope. Practically, this means that trauma is in the eye of the beholder. What is traumatic for one person may not be traumatic for another, and the body may experience trauma as a result of either a real threat or a perceived one.[3]

Other teams of researchers have reported that when an individual experiences an overwhelming or terrifying event, their natural threat response mechanisms are automatically deployed, causing a person to fight, flee, or freeze. These response mecha-

---

2. Judith Herman, *Trauma and Recovery: The Aftermath of Violence—From Domestic Abuse to Political Terror* (New York: Basic Books, 1992), 378.

3. Philip Browning Helsel, "Witnessing the Body's Response to Trauma: Resistance, Ritual, and Nervous System Activation," *Pastoral Psychology* 64 (2015): 681–93, https://doi.org/10.1007/s11089-014-0628-y.

nisms circumvent rational and logical thought and appeal to primal instincts in an attempt to keep one safe.[4] Still other research has concluded that human responses to threats are multidimensional, spanning the "biological, primitive, instinctual, and physiological, that is, [they are] subcortical in nature," rather than cognitive.[5] This means that trauma is determined by one's *response* rather than by a particular person, place, or thing.[6]

Simply put, trauma is subjective. Individuals vary significantly in their ability to handle various stressors, challenges, and overwhelming situations, based on a variety of factors such as genetic makeup, early environmental challenges, and attachment patterns. Even two siblings who grew up in the same home and were exposed to the same messages and experiences may respond to them in different ways. For example, when my mother told me about hell, my embodied response was one of fear and anxiety. But one of my siblings felt no such sense of urgency. This distressed me so much that I regularly witnessed to my sibling—to the degree that my mother told me I had to stop. What was overwhelming and stressful for me was not a problem for my sibling.[7]

---

4. Kristen L. Zaleski, Daniel K. Johnson, and Jessica T. Klein, "Grounding Judith Herman's Trauma Theory within Interpersonal Neuroscience and Evidence-Based Practice Modalities for Trauma Treatment," *Smith College Studies in Social Work* 86, no. 4 (2016): 377–93, https://doi.org/10.1080/00377317.2016.1222110.

5. Lina Grabbe and Elaine Miller-Karas, "The Trauma Resiliency Model: A 'Bottom-Up' Intervention for Trauma Psychotherapy," *Journal of American Psychiatric Nurses Association* 24, no. 1 (2018): 77, https://doi.org/10.1177/1078390317745133.

6. Laura E. Anderson, "The Living Experience of Healing the Sexually Traumatized Self" (PhD diss., Saybrook University, 2021), ProQuest (No. 28644488).

7. Anderson, "Living Experience of Healing"; Helsel, "Witnessing the Body's Response"; Peter Payne, Peter A. Levine, and Mardi A. Crane-Godreau, "Somatic Experiencing: Using Interoception and Proprioception as Core Elements of Trauma Therapy," *Frontiers in Psychology* 6, no. 93 (2015): 1–18, https://doi.org/10.3389/fpsyg.2015.00093; Babette Rothschild, *The Body Remembers*, vol. 2 of *Revolutionizing Trauma Treatment* (New York: Norton, 2017).

Trauma Responses and the Nervous System

When our bodies perceive a threat, the autonomic nervous system becomes activated and sends a signal to the sympathetic nervous system that danger is near and that it's time to fight or flee.[8] If neither of these responses are appropriate to the situation at hand (which is determined within a split second, deep in our subconscious mind), then the parasympathetic nervous system is engaged, which allows us to dissociate from the event. This reaction is commonly called freezing. In his research on healing CPTSD, Pete Walker introduced the trauma response of fawning. This is when an individual responds to a real or perceived threat by ingratiating themselves, trying to please, appease, and submit to evade danger.[9] This process happens in a matter of seconds and is embedded in our subconscious. Future events and experiences that are familiar trigger this same response, leading to retraumatization or trauma triggers.[10]

When the real or perceived threat has passed, the excess energy (such as adrenaline) that built up during the trauma experience must be released for a person to return to a calm state. This excess energy is often released from the body through trembling, shaking, crying, moaning, or screaming.[11] If the body is able to release this excess energy, then the individual's body and nervous system will not store it, and the trauma cycle is considered

8. Rothschild, *Body Remembers*.

9. Pete Walker, *Complex PTSD: From Surviving to Thriving* (Lafayette, CA: Azure Coyote, 2013).

10. Payne, Levine, and Crane-Godreau, "Somatic Experiencing"; Rothschild, *Body Remembers*; Bessel van der Kolk, *The Body Keeps the Score: Brain, Mind, and Body in the Healing of Trauma* (New York: Penguin Books, 2015); Bob Whitehouse and Diane Poole Heller, "Heart Rate in Trauma: Patterns Found in Somatic Experiencing and Trauma Resolution," Biofeedback 36, no. 1 (2008): 24–29, https://somaticexperiencing.dk/wp-content/uploads/2017/02/Bob-Whitehouse-Diane-Heller.pdf.

11. Helsel, "Witnessing the Body's Response"; Peter Levine, *Waking the Tiger: Healing Trauma* (Berkeley: North Atlantic Books, 1997); van der Kolk, *The Body Keeps the Score*.

complete.[12] However, if an individual can't release the excess trauma-related energy, then it is stored in the nervous system. Over time this can cause the psychological and physiological symptoms we often see in trauma survivors, such as hypervigilance, autoimmune disorders, social phobias, gastrointestinal disorders, relational issues, sexual dysfunction, anxiety, and depression. If an individual is unable to release trauma energy, then the brain's memory systems remain activated, prompting the body and nervous system to believe that the danger is ongoing and occurring in the present moment.[13]

In these instances, the limbic brain, which is responsible for detecting threats, is in full control and can rationalize any speech or behavior that will aid in safety. If trauma resided in our minds, it would be easy for the left, logical side of our brains to kick in and add a time and date stamp so that we could always remember, even when we are triggered, that whatever happened was in the past and is now over. But because of the way our nervous systems work, we experience trauma as timeless—that is, our nervous system is unable to differentiate between the past and the present. The trauma energy can get stuck in our bodies if we are unable to discharge it and come back to a felt sense of safety after a real, perceived, or remembered threat occurs. Practically, this means that when we are triggered, the nervous system believes that the past is now the present and reacts in a way that promotes survival. If this energy cannot be released it can become stuck inside the body and manifest in various physiological and psychological symptoms.

12. Helsel, "Witnessing the Body's Response"; Levine, *Waking the Tiger.*

13. Anderson, "Living Experience of Healing"; Peter Levine, Abi Blakeslee, and Joshua Sylvae, "Reintegrating Fragmentation of the Primitive Self: Discussion of 'Somatic Experiencing,'" *Psychoanalytic Dialogues* 28, no. 5 (2018): 620–28, https://doi.org/10.1080/10481885.2018.1506216; Moshe Szyf et al., "The Dynamic Epigenome and Its Implications for Behavioral Interventions: A Role for Epigenetics to Inform Disorder Prevention and Health Promotion," *Translational Behavioral Medicine* 6, no. 1 (2016): 55–62, https://doi.org/10.1007/s13142-016-0387-7; Bob Whitehouse and Diane Poole Heller, "Heart Rate in Trauma: Patterns Found in Somatic Experiencing and Trauma Resolution," *Biofeedback* 36, no. 1 (2008): 24–29.

According to van der Kolk, trauma involves experiencing physical sensations, emotions, and feelings in the present moment that are associated with experiences from the past. These sensations often cause a person to feel out of control, frightened, and uncertain.[14] In situations where external stimuli resemble the traumatizing experience, a person's body and mind begin to behave as if they are currently in a dangerous situation. They may experience flashbacks, behavioral responses (such as running away or becoming enraged), hypervigilance, and other trauma symptoms. These symptoms can overwhelm the body and brain and can leave an individual feeling as if they are continuously living in the past and unable to escape dangerous events.[15]

Since trauma is subjective, experiencing a scary, overwhelming, or dangerous situation does not mean that it will automatically result in trauma or a PTSD or CPTSD diagnosis. Remember my prior example: my nervous system perceived the threat of hell as dangerous and acted accordingly while my sibling's nervous system perceived it as nonthreatening.

In all situations, our bodies house the lived experience, and our brain, specifically our limbic brain, generates the *meaning* of this experience. Our prefrontal cortex (PFC), which is the part of our brain that is logical and does the thinking and reasoning, decides what to ignore, avoid, suppress, or acknowledge within the meaning that the limbic brain has created. This ultimately determines whether something is experienced as trauma. How the body stores an event, and the subsequent potential trauma, determines what an individual needs to recover.[16]

To sum up everything that you've just read, when asked "What is trauma?" I respond like this: trauma is not what happened to

14. Van der Kolk, *The Body Keeps the Score*, 24.
15. Anderson, "Living Experience of Healing."
16. Anderson, "Living Experience of Healing"; Helsel, "Witnessing the Body's Response"; Levine, Blakeslee, and Sylvae, "Reintegrating Fragmentation of the Primitive Self"; Rothschild, *Body Remembers*; Whitehouse and Heller, "Heart Rate in Trauma"; Zaleski, Johnson, and Klein, "Grounding Judith Herman's Trauma Theory."

you but your body and nervous system's *response* to what happened to you. Trauma is anything that is too much, too soon, or too fast and that undermines our normal ability to cope and return to a sense of safety. To reiterate, this means that trauma is *subjective*: what is traumatic for you may or may not be traumatic for me, and vice versa. It also means that trauma is *perceptive*: there does not have to be an actual threat or danger in front of you. The mere perception of threat and danger can feel threatening enough to overwhelm your nervous system. Finally, it means that trauma is *embodied*: trauma is stored in the body and not in the mind, which means that we cannot merely think trauma away.

Religious Trauma

Until the past few years, religious abuse and trauma were misunderstood and underexplored, leaving those who experienced such trauma confused about what was happening to them. Moreover, the treatment for healing from religious trauma often involved becoming an atheist or vilifying religion. While disavowing religion can be helpful for some, many people are distressed by the idea that in order to heal they have to reject their faith system. They rightfully recognize that this could easily become another form of fundamentalism. Further, the idea that religion is inherently harmful or will absolutely result in trauma or other mental health diagnoses is misleading. While involvement in specific religious groups and systems or instances of AREs are more likely to result in trauma, religion itself is not trauma.

Let's go back to the question "What is religious trauma?" *Religious trauma is trauma*. Just as the term "sexual trauma" helps us understand that an individual is resolving and recovering from an overwhelming or dangerous sexual situation, such as sexualized violence, religious trauma tells us that the trauma results from a single or multiple experiences that happened in a religious system or relationship. The word "trauma" in the term "religious trauma" refers to the same trauma that we discussed earlier in this chapter.

Religious trauma resides in our bodies and nervous systems in the same way that trauma from war, developmental trauma, or sexualized trauma live inside us. Though the triggers and environment of the original trauma may differ, how religious trauma lives in our bodies, on a physiological level, is the same.

Post-traumatic Stress Disorder (PTSD) and Complex Post-traumatic Stress Disorder (CPTSD)

Traumatology—the study, diagnosis, and treatment of trauma—is a relatively new and evolving field. If you were to ask any therapist how many trauma classes they took in their graduate program, you would be hard pressed to find someone who took more than one. I took my required crisis and trauma course in my first year of graduate school and despite the course title referring to both crisis and trauma, we mostly focused on crisis intervention. This is important to note as it is widely assumed that all therapists are trained in trauma care and can, therefore, treat it in their clients.

As mentioned earlier, the term "PTSD" did not appear in diagnostic manuals until 1980. In that era, trauma was still widely understood as an event, so diagnosis of PTSD was available only to those who had suffered harm from catastrophic events. As research continued and clinicians worked with traumatized clients, they met individuals who suffered symptoms similar to those who were diagnosed with PTSD. However, the event that caused those symptoms was not mentioned in the diagnostic criteria. So researchers began to develop language to categorize trauma, most notably "small t trauma" and "big T trauma." While the terminology was useful, it often created a sense of hierarchy, comparison, and expectation.

If someone suffered a big T trauma—that is, a trauma of catastrophic harm or alteration such as war, sexualized violence, natural disasters, or accidents—they were expected to suffer in prescribed and predictable ways. Small t traumas—such as interpersonal conflict, shame and humiliation, or legal trouble—were often thought of as lesser traumas that didn't necessarily require a PTSD diagnosis. Many researchers and clinicians recognized small t traumas as having prescribed symptoms and as being both developmental (happening in a person's childhood and adolescent years) and complex.

With such fixed categories, definitions, and symptoms for small t traumas and big T traumas, individuals can become confused as to why their experience of a big T trauma may not have resulted in the prescribed symptoms, and why many individuals who experience small t traumas have more intense symptoms, like those that typically characterize big T trauma. This often leads people to feel significant shame and to wonder if something is wrong with them.

I hear this often in online spaces and in my client sessions: "Nothing really big happened to me, so I can't be traumatized, but I am reacting as if I am." People often confuse religious abuse with religious trauma (we will discuss religious abuse and AREs in the next chapter). That is, many people believe that they will have religious trauma only if they have experienced abuse within a religious context. While it is true that abuse can result in trauma, the idea that it *must* result in trauma or that trauma can be caused only by abuse is false.

Though I don't like to categorize trauma, for the sake of ease it's appropriate to introduce the term "single incident trauma" (or "shock trauma") and to further discuss "complex trauma."

Single Incident Trauma

Single incident trauma is just that: trauma that results from a single incident or event such as a car accident, a natural disaster, or sexualized violence. One of the defining factors of a single incident trauma is that it has a before and an after. Before the incident, life was different; then something happened, and life changed. When I began doing EMDR therapy for panic attacks and flashbacks that I was having as a result of a physically and psychologically dangerous working environment, it involved specific incidences that had a clear before and after. My work experiences may not have been "catastrophic," a criterion for a PTSD diagnosis, but a year after leaving the job my symptoms fit the criteria. Single incident trauma is often considered easier to address than complex trauma, as trauma resolution usually involves discharging the excess trauma energy stuck in a client's body so that they can feel safe and stable again.

Complex Trauma

Complex trauma is, well, complex. I describe it as the result of experiencing consistent and pervasive threat or overwhelm without being able to escape. If someone is subjected to danger, abuse, neglect, overwhelm, or instability for long periods of time, it can lead them to live in survival mode or in a constant state of fight, flight, freeze, or fawn. Developmental trauma, domestic violence, war and terrorism, systemic racism and oppression, and cults are environments that can contribute to complex trauma.

For most people, one of the most difficult parts of complex trauma is that there was no "before and after." Rather, an environment of pervasive danger is often all that they know. In this case, a person may not even be able to remember a time prior to the abuse, neglect, danger, or overwhelm. In other cases, such as domestic violence, while a person may remember what life was like before the domestic violence began, these experiences are typically so overwhelming, intense, and psychologically terrorizing that they can alter a person's experience of the world.

People coming out of an HCR can have single incident trauma, complex trauma, or both. Single incident trauma within an HCR may result from things such as clergy sexual abuse, spiritual healings (or witnessing them), altar calls, rituals or practices, being publicly shamed or punished, or being excommunicated. These are considered single incidents because most of them have a before and an after. Unfortunately, many people who have suffered from single incident traumas within an HCR have been silenced, dismissed, or told it was simply a "bad church experience."

Religious Trauma as Complex Trauma

As I stated earlier, religious trauma fits into the category of complex trauma. For many individuals, growing up in an HCR was their normal. For me, there was never a time where I wasn't hearing about God, engaging in religious practices, or having my entire life defined by religious systems. There was no escaping it: I was a child, so there was nowhere I could go, and my parents and other caregiver figures were also promoting these messages in private and public, which meant that my caregivers and people who loved me were also the people who were enforcing rules and punishments for not abiding by the religious teachings. For many this means that the very people who are supposed to be a source of safety and stability are also a source of terror and confusion. Individuals who didn't grow up in this type of environment but joined later in life also might experience complex trauma as the dynamics of power and control are such that individuals are required to live, act, and think in a specific way or endure life-altering consequences.

Religious trauma is also complex in that it touches every area of life. HCRs require that more and more of your life be submitted to religious authorities and God. HCRs set rules for every area of life. The pervasive nature of an HCR often makes escaping from the system feel terrifying and nearly impossible.

Finally, religious trauma is complex trauma because a person experiencing it tends to live from a place of survival—especially if that person is a woman, a child, or another marginalized person. In the face of real or perceived threats, our brain and nervous system spring into action. If our nervous system determines that we can't fight or flee, it moves to fawning or freezing responses. A person with a fawning response lives in a state of needing to please, appease, or submit to avoid danger or punishment; a person with a freezing response often dissociates, becoming small, silent, and a nonparticipant in their life. It only takes a couple attempts at fighting or fleeing to realize that it's safer to fawn or freeze.

Treating complex trauma is hard because in many cases there is not one specific overwhelming incident. I have many clients who comb through the details of their lives trying to figure out *the thing* that happened to them. Many are dismayed when they are unable to point to one event, and they feel a sense of shame for the ways their body is responding. I submit, however, that religious trauma can result from many smaller but overwhelming and sometimes dangerous things that happen over time. It often takes my clients some time to let this sink in—it's okay if it takes you some time too. Again, trauma is not what happened to us but the way our nervous system *responded* to what happened to us. So even though nothing "big" happened in the HCR, the fear, overwhelm, danger, instability, and lack of safety took its toll.

Religious trauma is not a syndrome. There is no cluster of symptoms that every person with trauma has. While we can point to some symptoms as common, each person's nervous system, body chemistry, and internal landscape are different, so trauma symptoms will live in each person's body differently. I shared some of my symptoms in chapter 1. While some of you might identify with some or all of what I've experienced, it's more likely that you each have a unique set of symptoms. Complex trauma often results in a myriad of relational, physical, psychological, sexual, spiritual, and emotional difficulties and disorders that can feel all-encompassing and overwhelming. I encourage my clients not to get hooked on the list of symptoms they might find on the internet. Instead, I ask them to pay attention to what is happening inside them and to develop compassion toward themselves as they recognize that their bodies are trying to survive and protect them—even if those ways of survival are no longer useful or needed.

Understanding What Happened

When I first began understanding trauma and how it functions in the body, I had already been searching for years to understand what had been happening to me. By that point I had spent tens of thousands of dollars on doctors, therapists, healers, detoxes, health regimens, and any other obscure or hopeful treatment I could find that would help me deal with the enormous number of symptoms I was experiencing.

I was constantly discouraged when people told me that there was nothing wrong with me, that it was all in my head, and that I just needed to move on. But I couldn't deny what was happening in my body. So when I learned about trauma, I was elated— and furious. I was elated because for the first time I felt hope: I wasn't making this up in my head. Imagine that finding out I had CPTSD made me feel normal! But it did. I finally had a way to organize my experiences. I finally felt like I could do something about my pain.

I was also furious at the many helpers and healers I had worked with, paid, and trusted to help me. Despite them all hearing my story, not one of them ever suggested CPTSD. No one had taught me about my nervous system or about how trauma was stored in my body. Instead, I was offered guided meditation, supplements, referrals to other doctors, and cleanses to try to deal with all sorts of issues that weren't *the* issue.

Understanding trauma, validating my experiences, and being able to recognize the totality of what happened to me is what led to understanding my various diagnoses and symptoms, as well as long-term effects of the trauma. Understanding what happened to me—my experience in an HCR and other AREs—was an important part of my healing journey.

3

Religious Abuse and Adverse Religious Experiences

ABUSE, including religious or spiritual abuse, is different from trauma. Recall the definition of trauma from chapter 2: abuse is *what* happens to us, while trauma is our nervous system's *response* to what happens to us. Traditionally, abuse in the context of religious systems has been limited to experiences of clergy sexual abuse or ritualistic abuse that occurs in groups with extreme sacrificial or sexual practices. Certainly, these experiences are devastating, and there is a greater likelihood they will result in trauma. However, many other experiences that are not commonly understood as abuse still fit under the umbrella of abuse. Many people shy away from the term "abuse" to describe their experiences in religion. They fear not being believed or being told they are making too big a deal of their experiences.

Abuse is, at its core, the improper use or treatment of something or someone. In its most basic form, physical abuse is the improper use of one's body to harm another person's body. Sexual abuse is the improper use of sex against someone else. Religious abuse is the improper use of religious beliefs, teachings, doctrines, and relationships against another person. The word "improper" in this definition implies that there is a proper way to interact with others—a proper way to use one's body, to engage in sexual activity, or to practice religion.

Much of what is considered proper or improper is culturally defined. An emphasis on the cultural definition of proper and improper, and therefore abusive or non-abusive, has protected religion from scrutiny for centuries. Religion has traditionally been considered a protective and prosocial factor that helps individuals cope with distressing and harmful situations.[1] Because of this, religion's potential harmful effects have remained relatively untouched, as have the nuances of religion that lead to abuse and trauma. This means that many individuals' stories of religious abuse are dismissed, or the harmed individuals are given a reductive excuse: because humans are sinners, they are going to get it wrong and sometimes even hurt others, and such leaders or institutions should not be confused with a perfect, sinless God.

The abuse itself does not determine the long- or short-term impact and consequences. The impact of abuse is subjective, just as trauma is subjective. One person who has experienced religious abuse may experience confusion, anxiety, or depression. Another may experience extreme fear, hypervigilance, and social phobias. The impact of abuse depends in part on what happened (the actual experience of abuse) and in part on other factors. For instance, suppose a child experiences sexual abuse at the hands of a clergy member. Common symptoms of this experience may

---

1. Jung Yeon Lee et al., "Adolescent Risk and Protective Factors Predicting Triple Trajectories of Substance Use from Adolescence into Adulthood," *Journal of Child and Family Studies* 29, no. 2 (2019): 403–12, https://doi.org/10.1007/s10826-019-01629-9.

be withdrawal, confusion, isolation, anxiety, acting out their abuse toward others, and shifts and changes in attitudes, behaviors, and relationships. If the child has a strong support system around them, they may experience less severe symptoms or perhaps none at all. Another child may experience intense symptoms that get worse over time because those around them dismiss their story or do not notice the shifts in the child's behavior. While either or both children may experience trauma, the second child is more likely to experience trauma due to a lack of support and the dismissal of their symptoms.

Abuse doesn't require intentional malice or harm. This is important because in many cases religious abuse is an extension of what someone has been taught is normal, acceptable treatment and behavior. For individuals who have left HCRs, much of what we now consider abusive and harmful behaviors were first learned as spiritual practices, hierarchies, and disciplines, which were seen within the religious system as essential for living a godly life.

It's important to differentiate between abusive behaviors that occur from time to time for various reasons and an abusive system, relationship, or person in which ongoing abuse occurs as a result of power dynamics and control—although the former plays into the latter. I believe we are all capable of engaging in abusive behaviors, perhaps because of extreme stress, poor relational skills, modeling a caretaker's behavior, mental unhealth, or momentary lapses in judgment. My point is that we can engage in abusive behaviors that, once identified, can be changed so that patterns of abuse do not develop. One may engage in controlling behavior as a result of stress, continuation of modeled behavior, or to cope with trauma, but these behaviors may disappear naturally or with minimal attention as the root issues are dealt with. However, when patterns of abuse do develop, for whatever reason, the underlying dynamic shifts so that a person, group, or system has power and control over another.

Religious Abuse

Religious abuse is abuse administered under the guise of religion. It includes harassment, humiliation, mind control, psychological abuse, isolation, threats, intimidation, minimizing, denying, blaming, asserting spiritual authority, and making it difficult to leave the religious community. Religious abuse may also include misuse of religion for selfish, secular, sexual, or ideological ends. The following list identifies specific ways religion can be abusive.

- *Coercion and threats*: convincing individuals they must follow certain rules and lifestyles to secure their eternity, using threats to keep people from stepping out of line, threatening excommunication, making threats if an individual seeks help outside the religious institution, and making individuals drop or not seek to press charges for illegal behavior (such as, but not limited to, sexual abuse)
- *Intimidation*: making people feel afraid by using actions and gestures that could suggest disconnection from the community, teaching people they deserve eternal conscious torment if they do not subscribe to the system's rules, not valuing the safety of members by hiding or dismissing abuse
- *Emotional abuse*: making individuals feel bad about themselves, calling them names (e.g., calling them worthless or sinner), publicly or privately humiliating them for mistakes or acts deemed sinful, making them feel guilty, gaslighting them, teaching theology that promotes human worthlessness as a foundation of human existence, refusing to allow individuals to be autonomous and make choices for themselves
- *Isolation*: requiring individuals to have relationships only with people inside the religious system; requiring relationships with individuals not in the system to be cut off;

controlling what people do, who they talk to, what they read, or where they go; controlling access to information; using fear to justify actions (e.g., "people who do not believe like we do will try to get you to sin")

- *Minimizing, denying, and blaming*: making light of the requirement to be part of the system, not taking concerns seriously, shifting responsibility for abusive behavior, calling abusive behavior "sin issues" that require spiritual discipline instead of legal help, convincing an individual that they caused the abuse

- *Patriarchal privilege*: treating women, children, and other marginalized individuals as lesser than or subservient; placing only men in positions of authority, power, and leadership; allowing only men to define gender roles; using holy texts to justify abusive, oppressive, supremacist behaviors of men toward women, children, and marginalized bodies

- *Economic abuse*: preventing people from pursuing education, discouraging people from obtaining non-ministry job training or non-ministry careers, guilting people into giving the church money, keeping financial secrets (such as not permitting access to financial records), encouraging people to neglect the needs of their family in order to give more to the church or group, which may include messages such as "God will take care of all your needs"

These categories and specific behaviors and teachings are not exhaustive, but they give you an idea of the ways HCRs gain power and control. As I was understanding the correlations between domestic violence and dynamics of power and control within HCRs, I created a visual aid based on the Duluth Model's power and control wheel. I call this the religious power and control wheel, which can be viewed in the appendix near the end of this book.

Power and Control

I first learned about dynamics of power and control when I worked with clients who were in, trying to get out of, or had just gotten out of domestically violent relationships. These were not typical relationships ending in a bad breakup. Many of the victims developed symptoms of poor mental health and trauma because of these relationships. The Duluth Model's power and control wheel is a common tool used in working with people who have experienced domestic violence.[2] The wheel describes various behaviors that may initially seem benign or even common. However, researchers noticed that these behaviors, when occurring together and over time, created a dynamic in which one person gained power and control over another person. This often led to significant psychological distress and was foundational in relationships where physical and sexualized violence occurred.

Systems built on dynamics of power and control are abusive at their core. Within these systems is a hierarchy, typically built on patriarchy. At the top of this hierarchy is the leader(s) of the group who determines the roles, rules, and consequences and who—in the realm of high-control religions—is believed to be "called by God." This calling implies that followers will demonstrate submission and that the leader's words will not be questioned. Many systems also preach a message about the devil being actively at work in the world and wanting to tear down spiritual leaders. Many HCRs teach that suffering, being persecuted, and enduring hardships are either God's or the devil's way of testing you. This teaching creates a dynamic of silencing and suspicion as individuals who speak out about the leader(s) are often considered to be gossiping, persecuting the leader, or trying to stir up drama as an act of spiritual warfare. Concerns are dismissed or silenced.

2. I encourage readers to look online for images of the Duluth power and control wheel.

The leader(s) further perpetuates dynamics of power and control by creating rules for everyday living, relationships, spiritual practices, and how one must think and feel. These rules are underpinned by the idea that since God's mouthpiece dictated them, they should be viewed as spiritually sanctioned and are not to be questioned. Disregarding the rules is often an indicator of one's sinfulness, faithlessness, or rebellion. This can lead to accusations of being tricked by the devil, demon possessed, rebellious, unfaithful, prideful, or engaging in idolatry of self, which may lead to punishment, excommunication, or hell. In chapter 1, I shared the story of my relationship with my boyfriend, whom the church leadership did not approve of. They made rules for me and indicated that because they were my spiritual authorities, I had to listen. When I eventually decided to continue the relationship, I was called rebellious. Those who had power and spiritual authority then felt justified in how they treated me.

When dynamics of power and control are at play in a relationship or system, over time the person in the position of power strips the victim(s) of autonomy, voice, and choice. In the case of HCRs, it is easier for leaders to gain power and control because they appear to be backed by God, and they can wield the threat of eternal consequences. Add to this how many HCRs teach that humans are inherently sinful, that they cannot trust themselves, and that they will never choose good on their own. Individuals in these systems are primed to discard their minds, bodies, and sense of self in favor of the Bible, religious leadership, and God.

Often, clients will relay that their friends and family can't believe they could have "let" the abuse happen and ask, "Why didn't you just leave or speak up?" I remind my clients, however, that systems and relationships built on power and control follow a specific trajectory, one that is good at roping someone in and getting them to stay.

Love-Bombing

HCRs begin with love-bombing. Love-bombing is a period during which the perpetrator (an individual or a system) shows intense displays of affection, including giving compliments and gifts, seeking connection, and demonstrating a complete understanding of who you are. In this phase the victim (who does not know they are a victim) may feel belonging, connection, and understanding that they have longed for but never received. Victims often feel a sense of group camaraderie; are shown a romanticized version of God, Jesus, or other savior figures; and are told stories of how other group members were saved from sin, how they found purpose, and how good their life is now that they are a part of the group. Often when someone accepts a group's teachings or has a conversion experience, they feel a rush of emotions, and they feel different physiologically—perhaps lighter or more connected—as if they have tapped into a source greater than themselves. Other people in the group celebrate this phase, and the convert is given grace, patience, and attention as they begin their new life.

This phase in a relationship with a person or an HCR is important as this is what people look back on when times get tough. When tension, conflict, or confusion arise, many people do look back at this time and believe that if they could just change or get right with God, then life could return to how it was. Love-bombing in an HCR, like in an abusive relationship, hooks the individual on the receiving end of this attention. In a world where we long to feel connected and understood, the love-bombing phase speaks to very human needs and gives us hope that the things we have wanted most in life are finally coming to us.

Tension-Building Phase

The tension-building phase starts after the love-bombing phase begins to wane. Individuals may begin to experience greater pressure to conform to group standards. Patience and grace begin to dwindle for the group member who is figuring out how to live according to the rules. This is also a time where the ante is upped through isolating the victim and warning them that the outside world is a dangerous place. During this phase, questions are often met with more curtness and "because God says so" rather than the kind, patient answers given during the love-bombing stage.

During this stage, the victim begins to feel shame that they just aren't getting it. Sometimes they may even feel like they cannot accept the answers being given to them. However, this is often when memories are triggered from the love-bombing stage. The victim remembers how good it has felt to be part of the group, and they begin to blame themselves rather than asking questions about the group's requirements. Attempts to reason with other group members are squashed, and the individual may be punished by being accused of unfaithfulness or leading others to doubt that their salvation experience was real. This may cause even greater shame, and the individual may become even more compliant as they seek to prove that they are worthy of the group.

The different phases of this abuse cycle are often repeated with greater frequency and intensity the more the cycle goes around. What I described above might align best with a person's first experience of the tension-building phase. However, subsequent tension-building phases arise after honeymoon stages (described below) and might include disagreeing, feeling disillusioned, pushing back against leadership, requesting to see financial documents, maintaining relationships with people outside the group, using services that the group doesn't approve of (such as legal help or therapy), or engaging in behaviors that are considered forbidden or sinful. A person in the tension-building phase may also refuse to give more time, energy, or resources to the system, not heed advice or warnings from people in leadership positions, or not engage in spiritual practices and disciplines.

In the tension-building phase, people feel shame and confusion; it is often in this phase where autonomy and individual thought are challenged the most, and leaders make threats or demands to regain power and control. Statements such as "We are doing this for your own good" or "God has given us special insight into your life" are used to try to rein a person in to a more controllable position. Naturally, if the tension continues it leads to an explosion.

Explosion Phase

The explosion phase in a domestically violent relationship may include physical and sexual violence or other dangerous behavior. While this is not as common in HCRs, these things may occur. The explosion phase comes on the heels of tension building to the point where the person in question must be reined in at all costs or, in some cases, excommunicated from the church or system.

In HCRs, the explosion phase may occur in a public setting, such as membership meetings where various people's behaviors are discussed and sometimes consequences and punishments are voted on. This phase may include threats or active steps to excommunicate a person or cut them out of the group. This threat often coincides with warnings that the accused individual will no longer be under the protection of the church and instead will be at the mercy of the devil. The explosion phase may also happen in a more private setting and may involve harassment or isolation. In some cases, other members of the group are required to cease contact as a form of punishment.

In this phase, smear campaigns and misinformation may be spread along with accusations or threats, and a person might admit that they want to leave the group. In Scientology this is called "fair game": the defector is determined to be fair game for whatever natural or made-up consequences may come. The person is often followed and harassed, and online accounts may be hacked by group members attempting to maintain silence, power, and control. Regardless of what happens, this phase of the abuse cycle is messy and hurtful and leaves those on the receiving end of the explosion fearful of what might be taken away from them, such as community, positions, and support.

Honeymoon Phase

It may seem odd that the honeymoon phase comes on the heels of an explosion; however, the high emotion and intensity often grabs people's attention and causes them to prioritize reconciliation. Many people are eager to do whatever it takes to return to a safer status quo. Apologies and promises are made; some concerns might even be addressed. Placating statements used during the tension-building phase may be repeated (such as "We're doing this for your own good") but are often heard through a different lens as the person who has endured the explosion has also been convinced that they are, at least in part, responsible for what happened and that the leadership knows best.

This phase often involves a plan for the individual to be restored. Sometimes this includes an exhaustive list of tasks that someone may need to do to get back into the good graces of the group, and it is coupled with promises of connection and relationships like they used to have back in the love-bombing phase. Since an individual in this system is already conditioned to believe that they are inherently sinful and that they need people like religious leaders to help guide them, they are usually willing to go along with whatever restoration plans church leaders create for them.

Clients often describe this phase as the crazy-making phase. During this time, the person who perpetuated the abusive behaviors and caused the explosion makes statements that have a sliver of truth while also blaming the victim. Many clients reason that the grain of truth means that the entirety of the statement might be true, and they begin to wonder if they are going crazy, are to blame, or are actually the ones causing the abuse. However, these concerns are often downplayed or diminished as the person or system that caused the explosion is doing and saying all the right things, leading the victim to hope that life and relationships could be good again. Unfortunately, it is only a matter of time before tensions build again, and the cycle repeats itself.

Finally, it is worth noting that this cycle is also experienced by individuals who were born into HCRs. Like individuals who join the group after experiencing life outside the group, people who are born into HCRs may experience a love-bombing phase in their younger years as they are being taught about the foundations of the religion. For me, hell was always taught in relation to heaven. As scary as it was to hear about the idea of hell, I was taught about a wonderful gift I was given by Jesus dying on the cross for my sins and having assurance that I would go to heaven when I died. For many people who grew up in HCRs, the love-bombing phase would happen in tandem with encouragement to make professions of faith, participate in baptisms, or make commitments to God about various aspects of their life such as sexual purity, their money, or their time.

Why Didn't You Just Leave?

A common misconception of individuals in an HCR is that they are weak-minded, easy to manipulate, and willing targets. While HCRs may appeal to individuals who feel dejected or disconnected or who are hurting, many people are born into HCRs or are interested in them for other reasons, such as wanting to find purpose and community. Understanding how these groups operate allows us to also recognize that obtaining power and control over someone is not completely dependent on factors like age, gender, race, ability, socioeconomic status, or career.

Leaving a system like an HCR is much more difficult than opting to not go to church on a Sunday or a Wednesday. Consider some of the following characteristics of people in HCRs and why they might stay:

- *Arrested development*: Many individuals, especially if they are born into the HCR, suffer from arrested development

49

due to being indoctrinated into a specific way of living and believing, making leaving feel nearly impossible.

- *Inability to provide for themselves*: Many individuals do not have education or career skills outside of ministry that would make it possible to financially support themselves and/or their family if they leave.

- *Hopes, dreams, and possibilities*: During the love-bombing phase, victims of an HCR experience intense connection, relationship, and belonging. Many victims believe that if they could submit more, repent more, serve more, sin less, or become a stronger believer, then life might go back to the way it was. Additionally, HCRs often teach a certain expectation of suffering, that suffering and difficulty are God's way of testing and refining a person. When life gets difficult, it is not uncommon for members to see the difficulties as spiritually beneficial.

- *Denial*: Victims of HCRs may believe that since they have not experienced physical or sexual abuse their experience is not truly one of abuse, or they may believe that they need to trust God more and the leadership that God has placed over them. They may also believe that they are unable to trust themselves and their own instincts due to their inherent depravity.

- *Family, friends, and relationships*: Many people in HCRs have their entire relational and social support system within that group; leaving means they are required to give that up *and* enter the outside world alone. If someone does decide to leave, they are often confronted by people they love who may admonish them, challenge them, discourage them, or even question the person's salvation and eternal destiny to bring them back into the fold. Many people also feel significant grief and loss, which may feel too overwhelming to deal with.

- *Terrified of life outside the system*: Victims of HCRs have often been isolated and repeatedly taught of the danger and evils in the world outside of their system. Additionally, HCRs teach people what to think but not how to think, making it difficult for people to implement critical-thinking skills or even navigate everyday tasks.

- *Society's positive view of religion*: Since religion is considered a supportive factor in a person's life, leaving an HCR does not completely remove religion from someone's life. Due to our culture's generally positive view of religion, victims of HCRs may fear that others won't take them seriously (and may struggle taking themselves seriously). They may experience a lack of support, or they may not be believed.

Considering all these factors shows just how much courage it takes to leave a system like this. Contrary to what some popular pastors say, deconstruction is certainly not sexy.[3]

Adverse Religious Experiences

On an early morning Zoom call, I sat with three other therapists who specialize in religious trauma. Meeting with one another was a breath of fresh air. We had each felt isolated in our work, not sure if anyone else was treating religious trauma in the same way—from a body-based perspective and with the recognition that *religious trauma is trauma*. Prior to this, much of the literature and dialogue around religious trauma focused on two things: religious abuse and atheism as the cure for religious trauma. Many within the religious trauma community pointed out aspects of religious

3. See Milton Quintanilla, "Exvangelicals Criticize Matt Chandler for Saying People Find Christian Deconstruction 'Sexy,'" Christian Headlines, December 8, 2021, https://www.christianheadlines.com/contributors/milton-quintanilla/exvan gelicals-criticize-matt-chandler-for-saying-people-find-christian-deconstruction ism-sexy.

abuse and concluded that religion is inherently traumatizing. They noted that rejecting religion and embracing a life outside of it was a necessary part of healing. While that can be important for some people, the four of us agreed that for ourselves personally and for many of our clients, pointing out religious abuse was not the same as healing from religious trauma. In our experience, atheism didn't offer a cure for the deep, physiological, and psychological impacts of life in HCRs.

In 1998, Vincent Felitti published the Adverse Childhood Experiences Study (ACES) based on his work in an obesity clinic in the 1980s. He discovered that most of his clients had experienced childhood sexual abuse.[4] He continued to evaluate and assess his clients, collaborated with other medical professionals and researchers, and eventually developed the ACES questionnaire. The hypothesis of this questionnaire was that the higher the adverse childhood experience (ACE) score (on a scale of one to ten), the more likely it was that an individual's adult life would be affected by physical and mental health disorders. Felitti's study is still considered foundational to the treatment and understanding of trauma. Researchers such as Bessel van der Kolk and Judith Herman were able to use this data to further assert that the higher the ACE score, the more likely it was that developmental trauma, which was also considered interchangeable with CPTSD, would result.[5]

The ACE study led my colleague Brian Peck and me to come up with the hypothesis for adverse religious experiences (AREs). Brian and I cofounded the Religious Trauma Institute and (in collaboration with the Reclamation Collective) have hypothesized that the more AREs an individual has, the more likely they are

4. Vincent J. Felitti, "The Relation between Adverse Childhood Experiences and Adult Health: Turning Gold into Lead," *Permanente Journal* 6, no. 1 (2002): 44–47, https://www.ncbi.nlm.nih.gov/pmc/articles/PMC6220625.

5. Bessel van der Kolk, Alexander C. McFarlane, and Lars Weisaeth, eds., *Traumatic Stress: The Effects of Overwhelming Experience on Mind, Body, and Society* (New York: Guilford, 2007).

to experience various mental and physical health diagnoses. The greater the number of AREs, the more likely an individual is to experience religious trauma. Though formal research to support this hypothesis is still in the beginning stages, we have seen anecdotally that this is accurate.

To date, our working definition of AREs is as follows:

> Any experience of a religious belief, practice, or structure that undermines an individual's sense of safety or autonomy and/or negatively impacts their physical, social, emotional, relational, or psychological well-being.

This new term helps describe harmful experiences within religious systems without some of the traditionally understood stereotypes of religious abuse. Unlike in the ACE study, AREs are not categorized, nor is there an exhaustive list of experiences that are considered AREs. Researchers who have expanded the ACE study have recognized that it could be seen as reductive or incomplete since it suggests that only ten types of experiences are indicative of lifelong issues, including trauma.[6] We realize that even one ARE or ACE is enough for someone to experience lifelong issues, including trauma.

While this book doesn't contain every ARE, we will examine some of the AREs that are prevalent within high-demand/high-control environments.

Fear of Hell or Eternal Conscious Torment

I know I am not alone in my own experience with teachings about hell. Though many denominations and religions vary as to what someone must do to suffer eternal punishment, the foundation of this belief in Christianity is that humans are born sinful and

---

6. Canan Karatekin and Maria Hill, "Expanding the Original Definition of Adverse Childhood Experiences (ACEs)," *Journal of Adverse Adolescent Trauma* 12, no 3 (2018): 289–306, https://www.ncbi.nlm.nih.gov/pmc/articles/PMC7163861/.

need salvation. If a person accepts that Christ paid the penalty for humanity's sinfulness through his death on the cross, as evidenced by praying the sinner's prayer (and accepting the lifestyle and belief requirements), then heaven is guaranteed and hell can be avoided. Refusing to accept Jesus Christ as one's Lord and Savior will result in spending eternity in hell.

This can create panic, terror, and adversity because a person may have a constant sense of uncertainty about whether they are saved. People may shirk responsibilities and end up causing harm to others—such as not caring for their children or placing themselves in dangerous positions—to try to save people from hell because securing someone's eternal salvation is seen as more important than earthly matters.

Many of my clients experience "rapture anxiety." They were taught that Jesus is going to come back like a thief in the night and take his people to heaven. This belief was so deeply embedded that being home alone or not knowing where a parent or family member was caused significant panic and anxiety. They feared that their loved ones had been raptured, and they had been left behind. Many of my clients admit that the rapture is still the first thing that comes to mind when they find themselves alone when they don't expect to be.

Many people find themselves engaging in a form of obsessive-compulsive disorder (OCD) called "religious scrupulosity," which involves experiencing extreme anxiety around thoughts, words, and actions. They fear they have sinned or violated the tenets of their religion, often believing they'll go to hell for it. The fear of hell leads to extreme shifts in thoughts, behaviors, and relationships as they try to avoid eternal consequences.

Purity, Virginity, and Abstinence Culture

The messages, experiences, and impact of purity culture are some of the most damaging I see in my work. For the purposes of this book, "purity culture" encompasses the messaging from all religiously based movements that prioritize abstinence before marriage, virginity, and sexual purity and teach significant consequences for not abiding by such lifestyles.

Though many understand purity culture's message to be "Don't have sex before you are married," those who grew up in purity culture understand that the messages go far beyond this. Purity culture has also communicated messages about gender, sexuality, gender roles, modesty, lust, boundaries, consequences for sexual sin, racism or purity of race, and purity of mind and heart. It expects women to be the gatekeepers of men's purity of mind, heart, and body so that they do not sin. Women are taught that their bodies are dangerous; men are taught that their minds are.[7] Research has found that the messages of purity culture replicate messages of rape culture in that both focus on traditional gender roles, deny bodily autonomy (especially for women), are dehumanizing, are objectifying, put the responsibility on women to safeguard men's thoughts, lack consent, and blur lines between sexual sins (e.g., premarital sex) and rape.[8]

Purity culture often affects a person even after they have cognitively rejected its messages. Many individuals embody the specific teachings in ways similar to survivors of sexual abuse and assault.[9] As a survivor of sexual violence *and* purity culture, I was able to more easily resolve the trauma in my body stemming from my experiences of sexualized violence than from purity culture. While this is in part due to the differences between single incident trauma and complex trauma, it also shows how deeply adverse the messages of purity culture are.

7. Linda Kay Klein, *Pure: Inside the Evangelical Movement That Shamed a Generation of Young Women and How I Broke Free* (New York: Atria, 2018).

8. Kathryn R. Klement and Brad J. Sagarin, "Nobody Wants to Date a Whore: Rape-Supportive Messages in Women-Directed Christian Dating Books," *Sexuality & Culture* 21 (2016): 205–23, https://doi.org/10.1007/s12119-016-9390-x; Sarah Moon and Jo Regher, "'You Are Not Your Own': Rape, Sexual Assault, and Consent in Evangelical Christian Dating Books," *Journal of Integrated Social Sciences* 4, no. 1 (2014): 55–74.

9. Tina Schermer Sellers, *Sex, God, and the Conservative Church: Erasing Shame from Sexual Intimacy* (New York: Routledge, 2017).

Many individuals find that despite their cognitive rejection of purity culture, they are often faced with confusing, shameful, and frightening somatic responses as they engage with themselves and others in sexual ways.

Common responses can include the following:

- immense guilt and shame after sexual encounters
- extreme fear and panic around acknowledging and living out sexuality, gender, or gender roles outside prescribed definitions
- physical pain and/or aversion to sexual activity
- fear of hell for engaging in sexual acts
- confusion, shame, and blame when a partner does not live up to the expectations and definitions of their gender as they were taught by purity culture
- self-disgust
- distrusting oneself and others
- unwanted pregnancies (due to lack of knowledge about birth control or fear of punishment for pregnancy termination)
- sexually transmitted diseases and infections (due to lack of sexual education)

Altar Calls, Healings, and Scary Sermons

When I was a freshman in high school, I went to a youth conference. In a jam-packed auditorium on a Saturday night, the speaker gave a strongly worded, persuasive, and charismatic talk about our need for Jesus, about sexual purity, and about being on fire for God. At the end he invited us to close our eyes for prayer while he admonished us to recommit our lives to God. Though I was certain I was a Christian, I knew this recommitment process was something I was supposed to do. I also knew that the recommitment meant I would have to give up my crush at school since he wasn't a Christian. I didn't want to do this. In a bold move of rebellion, I told God a firm "no way" and tuned out the remainder of the sermon.

Sermons or messages like this are common in HCRs. These are powerful talks that evoke emotion, fear, and action to get individuals to commit further not only to God but also to the group.

Depending on the church or denomination of the HCR, a person may hear variations of the same message from pastors, leaders, and other spiritual authorities. Often the speaker's position of power is enough to cause fear in the parishioner (especially if the parishioner is a child!) because HCRs also teach that the leader is a person God has ordained. On top of that, messages from leaders are often filled with rhetoric about ultimate truth that is seen as proof of God's existence, even if it goes against a person's lived experiences. Some more charismatic denominations engage in healings, prophesying, giving a "word" from the Lord, being slain in the Spirit, dancing or laughing for God, finding gemstones from heaven, and other spiritual practices that may result in an individual feeling overwhelm in the moment.

Many of my clients disclose that these experiences left them with a sense of having no autonomy or boundaries; fear of authority; belief that they could not trust themselves; fawning responses; confusion over experiences; significant medical conditions due to the belief that God would heal them through their pastor, and therefore they didn't need medical care; loss of funds and financial resources due to supporting different ministries, churches, and spiritual leaders; pervasive feelings of guilt and shame; feelings of powerlessness and helplessness; extreme fear for their soul or the souls of others; and much more.

Though many folks can easily identify dynamics of power and control in these situations and reject the words and practices of various spiritual leaders and groups, they also acknowledge that these singular or collective experiences affected them during the remainder of their time as part of a religious group. And those who have left still feel the effects.

Spanking and Corporal Punishment

The American Academy of Pediatrics states unequivocally that there is never any situation in which spanking a child leads to positive results.[10] Even still, many individuals in HCRs engage in spanking and other forms of corporal punishment and justify it by pointing to the Bible.[11] One particular verse in the Bible, Proverbs 13:24, is often used to support this type of punishment. Though translations of this verse differ slightly, they communicate a similar message: "He who fails to use a stick hates his son, but he who loves him is careful to discipline him" (Complete Jewish Bible); "Whoever refuses to spank his son hates him, but whoever loves his son disciplines him from early on" (God's Word).

If an adult hits another adult, there are severe consequences, often including long-lasting legal ramifications, but religion does not encourage the same common sense in parent-child relationships. Though children have no way to protect themselves and though misbehavior is often the result of a dysregulated nervous system, within many religions it's acceptable to assault a child as a form of punishment meant to teach them how to be a good human being.

Individuals who experienced spanking or corporal punishment at the hands of their caregivers may balk at using the term "physical assault" to describe such practices. And yet when given space to accurately and honestly describe these experiences, one may find that the long-lasting impacts are numerous. Research indicates a connection between children who were spanked or who

10. "AAP Says Spanking Harms Children," American Academy of Pediatrics, 2018, https://www.aap.org/en/news-room/news-releases/aap/2018/aap-says-spanking-harms-children/.

11. Robert D. Sege and Benjamin S. Siegel, "Effective Discipline to Raise Healthy Children," *Pediatrics* 142, no. 6 (2018), https://doi.org/10.1542/peds.2018-3112.

received corporal punishment and those who commit assault later in adulthood.[12] Spanking also correlates with mental health issues later in life.[13] Many of my clients who experienced spanking or corporal punishment more easily accept abusive behaviors within relationships, including physical abuse from an intimate partner, than clients who have not experienced spanking or corporal punishment. They had learned that physical abuse and assault was the normal punishment for making someone upset or angry. This led them to engage in repeated adult romantic relationships that were characterized by various forms of abuse.[14]

One client who had experienced corporal punishment as a child told me they recognized the pattern of abuse in their subsequent relationships after leaving the family home. Though they never engaged in abusive behaviors toward others, they consistently found themselves in relationships—platonic, friendships, collegial, and romantic—that included dynamics of power and control. In some relationships they experienced instances of physical abuse, though none were "as bad" as what they had experienced in childhood. Consequently, they considered these instances of physical abuse and assault in their adulthood to be nonconsequential instead of a red flag. The client made a passing comment about the assaults being a normal part of a loving relationship.

Unable to contain myself, I asked, "I'm curious to know if your definition of love includes abuse and assault?"

They looked at me with a serious yet fearful face and asked, "Is that not a part of love?"

12. Murray A. Strauss and Carrie L. Yodanis, "Corporal Punishment in Adolescence and Physical Assaults on Spouses in Later Life: What Accounts for the Link?," *Journal of Marriage and the Family* 58, no. 4 (1996): 825–41.

13. Afifi et al., "Spanking and Adult Mental Health Impairment: The Case for the Designation of Spanking as an Adverse Childhood Experience," *Child Abuse and Neglect* 71, (2017): 1999.

14. Afifi et al., "The Relationship between Harsh Physical Punishment and Child Maltreatment in Childhood and Intimate Partner Violence in Adulthood," BMC Public Health, May 23, 2017, https://bmcpublichealth.biomedcentral.com/articles/10.1186/s12889-017-4359-8.

For many weeks after, we processed how their definition of love had come to involve abuse and how this had impacted most areas of their life.

Patriarchy and Oppression

Very few people have experienced a nonpatriarchal culture. Patriarchy, to greater and lesser degrees, is baked into our cultures, societies, religions, families, and relationships. Patriarchy is the belief that one person or one type of person is at the top of a hierarchical ladder and that this person determines our ways of thinking and relating in every area of life. In the patriarchal culture in which we live, men (most notably cisgender, heterosexual, white men) are at the top of this hierarchy and make the decisions, hold power, create rules, determine moral authority, hold social privilege, and control property. In my opinion patriarchy is at the root of racism, capitalism, misogyny, ableism, and sexism. It is the foundation of oppression.

Within many HCRs, patriarchy is also recognized as the way that God ordered creation. Religious authorities note that in Genesis, God created Adam first and then created Eve out of Adam. This means that men are the natural leaders and women are second in command. White American evangelicalism expands this hierarchy by using gender, sexuality, and skin color to determine the power and authority one holds within the system. For instance, in the evangelical patriarchal system, men have authority over women. However, white men have more power than men of color. White women, though holding lesser authority than men, have more authority than women of color. Additionally, individuals who deviate from a cisgender and heterosexual identity are stripped of power. They are often told that identifying this way is sinful or impossible.

Although a religious group may not overtly discriminate against a person with a disability, it is not uncommon for able-bodied individuals to be prioritized while disabled persons are told to rejoice in their suffering, are used as props, and may even be told that their disability is a result of sin. Rather than seeing a disabled person as an individual, religious systems often make no effort to include them.

In a patriarchal system, no one wins. Though it would appear that a cisgender, heterosexual white man has the upper hand, this should not be mistaken as "winning." I work with many individuals who hold this identity who have been deeply wounded by religious patriarchal standards and who experience great pain and remorse for having inflicted and lived out those patriarchal standards in ways that have oppressed others.

Oppression from patriarchy wounds individuals at their core. Identities are stripped, humanity is extinguished, liberation is denied, and survival feels difficult. Many individuals struggle to acknowledge and validate their unique identities and those of others. People are pitted against one another. Humanity lives in survival mode—fearful that equality for those lower on the hierarchical ladder will mean oppression for them.[15] This leads to long-term effects far greater than we have space for here. This, too, is an ARE that impacts each of us in unique ways.

THIS LIST OF AREs IS NOT EXHAUSTIVE; as you can see, it's not specific either. There simply isn't space in one book to list every ARE I have come across. And I think it's best that I don't. Why? Because I do not want to be the determiner of what an ARE may have been for *you*. If your experience was adverse, then *it was adverse*—regardless of whether it made its way onto an arbitrary list written by a white woman in the South. Your experience is valid, and it matters. And if it included pain and adversity or resulted in trauma, then I am so sorry it happened to you.

15. Resmaa Menakem, *My Grandmother's Hands: Racialized Trauma and the Pathway to Mending Our Hearts and Bodies* (Las Vegas: Central Recovery Press, 2017).

In closing this section on AREs, I want to reiterate that an ARE is just that: an experience. It's a thing or an event. It's not trauma. But it could result in trauma. While research is ongoing, we suspect that the more AREs an individual endures, the greater the likelihood that the result will be religious trauma. This is not to say that "only" one ARE would not result in trauma or that one hundred AREs will absolutely result in trauma. Remember: trauma is subjective, perceptive, and embodied. Regardless of whether your experiences result in trauma or something else, what happened to you should *not have happened.*

4

Nervous System 101

PRIOR TO MAKING THE COMMITMENT to accept Jesus into my heart, I struggled with sleeping. I was terrified that Jesus would come back in the middle of the night and that I wouldn't get to go to heaven. As a result, I panicked when I went to bed. My heart would race, and it felt like there was an elephant sitting on my chest. My parents would tell me to trust in the Lord. They even taught me a song that had the line "when I am afraid, I will trust in You," which I would sing over and over, hoping that it would calm my panicky little body down. When I was finally allowed to ask Jesus into my heart, my problems with sleeping ceased. I had the assurance I needed that if Jesus came back, I would be taken to heaven and spend eternity with the people I love the most. Though I never became the type of person who could fall asleep in a matter of seconds (a superpower I deeply wish I had!), even if I wasn't able to fall asleep, it was not due to panic or anxiety over being consigned to life without my family.

Until I began deconstructing my religion.

Instantly and subconsciously, I started panicking when I would crawl in bed at night. Though it took me years to realize that this was exactly how I felt as a child, I knew something was wrong. Sleep became excruciating as my mind began to race, and even prescribed sleeping medicine didn't help me fall or stay asleep.

I came to realize that my nervous system believed that it was terrifying, even life-threatening, to go to sleep without assurance of eternal salvation and thus I had become fearful of being left alone without the people I loved. The fears of my childhood were occurring again in the present moment. I was often restless and would wake up several times during the night. I tried guided meditation, hypnosis, and bedtime routines, and while they would sometimes help, sleep was still difficult because my body perceived sleep as scary.

Understanding the Nervous System

We are going to jump into a bit of science. By understanding the nervous system and how it functions within the body, I hope you might be able to understand yourself and your experiences better, feel increased self-compassion and decreased shame, and have some tools for resolving religious trauma.

The nervous system is our body's command center—think of a motherboard from *Star Trek*. The nervous system originates in the brain and controls everything we do, including breathing, body temperature, movement, thinking, and feeling; it controls our automatic responses and the various systems of our body, such as our digestive and immune systems. The nervous system is made up of our brain, our spinal cord, and all the nerves in our body; our nerves carry messages to and from our body and brain so that we can take in the information around us and respond accordingly.

The Vagus Nerve

The vagus nerve is the longest nerve in the nervous system. It begins at the base of the brain (the brainstem) and wanders throughout the body, connecting with many of our body's visceral organs. The vagus nerve's pathways are bidirectional, meaning that this nerve sends information from the body to the brain and from the brain to the body. What makes this nerve unique, however, is that 80 percent of the nerve fibers send information from the body to the brain. The other 20 percent of the nerve fibers enable our brain circuits to change our physiology dynamically and dramatically in a subconscious and quick way—like causing our heart to beat slower or faster.[1]

The vagus nerve is divided into two parts: the upper half is called the ventral vagal complex and connects to our heart, lungs, pharynx, and larynx. This part of the vagus nerve helps us feel safe in the social context around us, helps us communicate and connect with others, and creates a sense of homeostasis (or status quo) within our bodies. The bottom part of the vagus nerve, which begins at the diaphragm and moves downward is called the dorsal vagal complex and connects to the stomach, liver, spleen, kidney, colon, and intestines.[2] Essentially, this part of the vagus nerve is responsible for our calm state; it slows our heart rate, stimulates our gut for digestive purposes, and helps us return to a calm state where we can grow and restore. This is known as the parasympathetic nervous system (PNS).

The sympathetic nervous system (SNS) branches off of the vagus nerve, and it regulates our breathing, heart rhythms, blood flow and pressure, and body temperature. The SNS is also what is initially activated when we sense a real, perceived, or remembered threat. The SNS moves us toward fight or flight responses. The SNS works with the ventral vagal complex to give us energy for our daily life activities.[3]

---

1. Deb Dana, *Polyvagal Flip Chart: Understanding the Science of Safety* (New York: Norton, 2020); Stephen W. Porges, *The Pocket Guide to the Polyvagal Theory: The Transformative Power of Feeling Safe* (New York: Norton, 2017).

2. Dana, *Polyvagal Flip Chart.*

3. Dana, *Polyvagal Flip Chart.*

These two branches of the nervous system—the PNS and SNS—form what we will refer to as the autonomic nervous system (ANS). When an individual is in a safe situation or environment, the ANS registers that in the body by keeping it in a calm state. However, when real or perceived danger is on the horizon, the ANS also can move the body into a more activated or mobilized state. For instance, when the ANS senses threat, the body activates organs and parts of the brain—such as the hypothalamus, pituitary gland, and adrenal glands—in order to create cortisol and adrenaline, which give us additional energy to fight or flee; simultaneously it suppresses digestive functions like hunger or needing to use the bathroom, since, in the face of danger, it is inconvenient to have to stop to eat or go to the bathroom![4]

Neuroception

One other term that's important to know is "neuroception," which is "the process through which the nervous system evaluates risk without requiring awareness."[5] Neuroception is an automatic and subconscious process that involves various areas in our brain scanning our environment and communicating whether we are safe or in danger. If a threat is detected, our physiological state begins to shift to give us the best chance for survival. Since this is a subconscious process, we are not aware of neuroception, but we feel its physiological shifts (known as interoception). This is better known as a gut-level intuition or a feeling or sensation that something is happening. Although neuroception is meant to protect us and help us survive, it is not always accurate; sometimes neuroception detects risk when there is none.[6]

Neuroception is often connected with the things that trigger us. The process of neuroception requires scanning for danger 24/7 and does not operate on logic or rational thought. It is based on

---

4. Dana, *Polyvagal Flip Chart*; Porges, *Polyvagal Theory*.
5. Porges, *Polyvagal Theory*, 19.
6. Porges, *Polyvagal Theory*.

sensation and familiarity or remembering, even if the remembering is not conscious. This means that if the part of your brain that is scanning for danger (often referred to as the reptilian brain) notices something familiar (e.g., a scent, a tone of voice, a facial expression), it quickly returns its sensorial memory to the previous time that you came across that tone, expression, or scent. If this earlier memory is connected to danger or threat, the reptilian brain automatically assumes that what is in front of you is also a threat and acts accordingly, preparing your body to fight, flee, freeze, or fawn.

I live in the South, where many places, even public spaces, play Christian music. Many years ago, as I was running errands, a particular song came on in the store and within moments I was sweating, my stomach was upset, and I had the urge to drop all the things I had in my arms and run out. Instead, I quickly made my purchase and left the store. As I sat in my car trying to regulate my breathing, I tried to figure out what had just happened. On reflection, I recalled that this song was playing in the background of an experience I had in which two older women from my former church were rebuking me and trying to cast demons of deceit out of me. I had felt trapped and unable to leave the room, dissociating until the experience was over. Though that experience happened years ago, my reptilian brain associated the song with a terrifying time and through neuroception assumed that it was happening again.

The Ventral Vagal Complex and Social Engagement

Before we discuss the nervous system and trauma, we must further explore the ventral vagal complex. The ventral vagal complex is responsible for what is called the social engagement system (SES). The SES is our first layer of protection when a real or perceived threat arises.

Imagine a toddler is at the playground with her mother. With her mother close by, the toddler ventures onto the various equipment.

As she tries climbing, her fingers get pinched, and she starts to cry. The toddler scans the playground looking for her mother. When the toddler sees her, she stretches her arms out, asking for her mom to pick her up and comfort her. The mother might sit with the child for a few moments, rocking her back and forth, speaking softly and telling her that everything will be okay. Then, as if nothing has happened, the child begins to squirm, indicating she is ready to head back to the playground.

This is an example of the SES, which we engage with for our entire life, even when our parents aren't there to hold us, rock us, and make sure everything is okay. As adults, we engage with our senses in social situations by becoming attuned to facial expressions, noises, tone, cadence, and gestures that help us recognize if the situation around us is safe and calm or dangerous. When our nervous system detects danger (again, real, perceived, or remembered) not only do our senses become hyper-attuned to help us take in our surroundings but we might also look for ways within our social system to remember that we are safe. For instance, we might reach for our phone to text or talk to a friend, we might call out for help, or we might yell. In some cases, we might look for crowds of people to surround ourselves with as more people may provide a greater sense of safety. Our SES helps us detect a sense of welcome or warning signals in the environments around us.

Trauma and the Nervous System

Remember, trauma is the nervous system's response to anything that is too much, too soon, or too fast in which our capacity to cope and return to a sense of safety is inaccessible. Judith Herman, Peter Levine, and Bessel van der Kolk agree on this definition and add that trauma is in the eye of the beholder.[7] They note that

7. Judith Herman, *Trauma and Recovery: The Aftermath of Violence—From Domestic Abuse to Political Terror* (New York: Basic Books, 1992); Peter Levine, *Waking the Tiger: Healing Trauma* (Berkeley: North Atlantic Books, 1997); and

when the nervous system perceives long-lasting or inescapable events or experiences as overwhelming, or when processing what happened is not possible, our bodies respond with physiological and psychological symptoms that become protective or coping measures. However, if these symptoms become chronic, then the body begins to create additional patterns of living that lead to a state of constant dysregulation.

Over time, as these experiences pile up, our bodies and nervous systems live in a constant state of "on" or "off" and subsequently learn that the body is not a safe place to be. Combine that with the messages that many HCRs preach (see chap. 3 under "Adverse Religious Experiences"), and in addition to being unsafe the body becomes a place of shame. However, if we disconnect, or dissociate, from the body it is still affected. Even when we dissociate, our body continues to pile up the overwhelming experiences and bear the burden of what is happening to us.

Each body stores these events differently and has different physiological and psychological symptoms. No matter how each body presents, research is beginning to recognize that many symptoms are alleviated or reduced with minimal effort and attention when trauma, as the root issue, is addressed.

It is important to understand our nervous system so that we can understand the role it plays in trauma. This, in turn, will help us understand not only religious trauma but also how it affects us, even after deconstruction or deconversion.

Take a moment to notice your surroundings right now. Slowly glance to the left and right, in front of you and behind you, and let your eyes take in the environment. As you scan your surroundings, notice if anything helps you feel a sense of calmness in your body. This may feel like a sense of spaciousness in your body, ease in taking deeper breaths, your shoulders or neck relaxing, a

---

Bessel van der Kolk, *The Body Keeps the Score: Brain, Mind, and Body in the Healing of Trauma* (New York: Penguin Books, 2015).

smile creeping onto your face, or a pleasant sigh. Notice also if you take in something that comes with a sense of warning, such as anxiety in your belly, a quickening heart rate, tension or resistance in your body, or feelings of numbness. Take note of that and continue scanning your environment until you find something that signals welcome. Allow your gaze to rest there until your body starts to relax.

Fight, Flight, Freeze, and Fawn Responses

As discussed above, if our nervous system is unable to find solace within our social environment, the SNS branch of the vagus nerve becomes activated and our body secretes various hormones, such as adrenaline and cortisol, to engage our fight, flight, freeze, or fawn responses. This process happens subconsciously in a split second. When a threat enters the picture, we do not rationally think through our options. Instead, our nervous system begins determining if we can intimidate the threat (fight), get away from the threat (flight), appease the threat (fawn), or make the threat lose interest (freeze).

When a real, perceived, or remembered threat is detected, our nervous system first defaults to either a fight response or a flight response. If neither of these are options, our nervous system moves us into more primitive, smaller responses such as fawning and freezing. For many women and children, especially those in HCRs, fawning and freezing are often the only two responses available because the patriarchal hierarchy of an HCR does not afford women or children the resources to fight or flee. As mentioned above, a fawning response may involve pleasing, appeasing, and submitting to another person. While in the long term this may present as codependency, the motivation behind fawning is survival. The nervous system has determined that meeting others' needs, making oneself smaller, doing what others want, and reassuring others will provide safety.

Our nervous system engages the freeze response when it recognizes that fighting, fleeing, or fawning are unavailable. Freezing often looks like being quiet and hiding. While a person who is in freeze mode appears quite small, shallow, and still, underneath the surface there is significant activation. Imagine having your foot on the gas pedal and the brake pedal at the same time—that's what is happening when someone is in freeze mode. On the surface a person may appear to be pushing the brake pedal, but beneath the surface, their SNS is pushing the gas. The SNS is activated, looking for the moment when fight or flight can be reengaged. We've discussed the parts of the brain that determine threat and our response to it. But humans also have developed a prefrontal cortex (PFC), which is the part of the brain that oversees rational thought, cognitive processing, habit making, and thinking. While this part of the brain serves us in our everyday life, when threat or danger comes, it shuts down, leaving the nervous system in charge.

Once a threat has passed, our PFC starts to reengage and, with it, our cognitions and meaning-making abilities. Instead of letting our bodies go through the natural process of discharging excess trauma energy that has been created, our thinking brain reengages and tells us "Oh, that wasn't so bad," "I can't believe I made such a big deal over nothing!" and other statements that help us make sense of what transpired.

This is how trauma gets stuck in the body—which makes it nearly impossible to feel safe inside our bodies and in the world. Even though we may cognitively know that we are safe or that the danger has passed, we begin to live in a place of constant hypervigilance and activation, often believing the world is a cruel, painful, and judgmental place.

High-Control Religions and Trauma

Though religious trauma is an emerging clinical field, simply recognizing that religious trauma is trauma is helpful. When religious trauma is recognized as trauma the same way other experiences resulting in trauma are recognized as trauma, it means we have a wealth of research and interventions at our fingertips.

Looking at HCRs through the lens of the nervous system will help us understand the physiological impact of the teachings and practices. Neither religion nor its practices and beliefs are inherently traumatic; rather, the effect of an experience, belief, or practice on an individual is specific to that person. How your nervous system responded, or still responds, to various religious teachings, beliefs, and practices is both unique and valid, regardless of how others were affected.

Physiologically speaking, our SNS is designed to turn on and off as needed. The SNS has many other functions outside of activating fight and flight responses when we are in dangerous situations. The energy that we use to run away from danger is the same energy source we tap into when we are running a race or exercising. However, even in the case of what would seem to be a healthy, supportive activity (like exercise), our bodies are not meant to maintain that level of energy and activation forever. Yet traumatized individuals are often stuck in this "on" state; they can be stuck in an "off" state too. Whether we are stuck in an "on" or "off" state, trauma results and our body begins to see long-term physiological and psychological impacts.

Stuck in an "On" State

The tenets of many HCRs are a recipe for constant SNS activation. Many of the clients I have worked with were taught some iteration of these messages:

"The Devil is out to get you; always be on guard."

"We are in a spiritual war; we must be ready to fight at any moment."

"Watch out because the people on the outside [the world] are looking for any opportunity to pull you down."

"You must always be moving forward, or you are backsliding."

While these messages may seem benign, and certainly may have been for some, they also require a type of hypervigilance. The call to fight or flee is embedded within these messages. Additionally, many HCRs encourage and require activity rather than rest; rest is often seen as necessary only for those who are not relying on God for their strength and for every need. HCRs thrive on keeping adherents in a state of activation so that they are ready for spiritual battles.

When an individual is in a constant state of arousal or activation, they assume the posture of either fight or flight; they are on the defensive, prepared to be attacked. Take a moment and reflect on the last time you were in a defensive posture. Perhaps you were heatedly debating someone, trying to set a boundary, standing up for yourself, or actively defending yourself from danger. Think about yourself in that space. In those moments of SNS activation, were you able to think calmly or rationally? Were you able to consider others' viewpoints or opinions? Were you able to give others the benefit of the doubt? Most likely, the answer is no. When our SNS is activated due to real, perceived, or remembered danger, our rational, thinking brain is offline, and our nervous system is concerned with one thing: survival.

This is often helpful to recognize both when you reflect on how you felt and acted in an HCR and when trying to understand those still in that system. Many people grew up believing that those outside of the religious system were enemies, which meant they were dangerous and threatening, something one would need to defend against. This permitted group members to engage with enemies from that defensive posture, instead of seeing them as people who were simply seeking human connection. Those inside HCRs still believe that they are misunderstood and persecuted and that the world is out to get them. They see the world as evil, a spiritual battleground. This is often why it can feel impossible to dialogue with others and sometimes even to engage in relationships altogether after leaving that religious system.

Another feature of staying in constant SNS activation is that our nervous systems perceive anything that is different as dangerous. Most HCRs teach that anything outside of their system is meant to tear you away from your intended purpose. This creates fear toward humans and relationships outside of the system, and toward values, thoughts, and decisions that are not in line with the system. When our SNS system is activated, it doesn't do a great job of differentiating between major and minor dangers. Danger is danger, so whether a person is discussing political candidates, music, deeply held values, or atonement theories, any difference of opinion or value can seem, to the activated SNS, in need of defending and protecting. This is often why we see many people in HCRs demanding that others believe the exact same way they do. This demand typically comes not from a place of wanting to control others but from a deep need to feel safe. And sameness feels safe.

Stuck in an "Off" State

Not everyone in an HCR is stuck on "on." Some people are stuck on "off." These people appear quiet and submissive and seem to want to keep the peace. Many factors can contribute to this (gender, previous experiences, and relational factors), but while they may appear "off" on the outside, the SNS system is "on" on the inside. People in this "off" state often demonstrate very little pushback and do not seem easily angered. They are the people others might be shocked by when they explode in anger or do something that seems out of character before going back to their quiet, submissive stance.

Living in a constantly activated state can be damaging. However, many people don't notice it or write off their symptoms as spiritual warfare, God testing them, or areas where they need to repent. For example, I didn't recognize how activated my SNS was until I was out of the church and felt the difference because externally I presented as being in an "off" state. When I was in an HCR, I had anxiety daily. I was nearly incapacitated by the smallest decisions because I was terrified that if I made the wrong choice, then God's will for my life would be thwarted. My anxiety, however, was also a source of shame because it revealed my lack of trust in God. Despite praying, listening to worship music, reading my Bible, and engaging in spiritual practices, my anxiety subsided only temporarily. When it came back, so did the shame.

Potential Long-Term Effects of HCRs on the Nervous System

Over the years I have reflected on who I was during my decades in an HCR, and the toll it took is staggering. An abundance of research recognizes the long-term effects of a nervous system that is stuck on "on" or "off." Chronic fatigue, chronic pain, autoimmune disorders, sexual dysfunction, social phobias, OCD, depression, anxiety, relational issues, gastrointestinal issues, and diagnoses such as PTSD and CPTSD are common among individuals who have experienced chronic nervous system dysregulation and religious trauma.[8]

When I discussed religious trauma as a form of complex trauma earlier, I indicated that trauma resolution often looks different for those with complex trauma than those with single incident trauma. One of the more pervasive issues I see in complex trauma survivors is the magnitude and quantity of triggers. That said, many people experience great relief when they realize that living as a healing person does not mean that they won't be triggered. Healing, instead, means that *when* you are triggered, you have access to different coping mechanisms. Religious trauma survivors

---

8. Laura E. Anderson, "The Living Experience of Healing the Sexually Traumatized Self" (PhD diss., Saybrook University, 2021), ProQuest (No. 28644488).

will be triggered. Sometimes it will happen frequently and feel intense. Sometimes triggers will pop up after being dormant for a long time. Other times a trigger will catch someone off guard because they had no idea that it would be a trigger. What I've found, though, is that when all of life is immersed in an environment that requires constant high alert and being on guard, everything can feel scary.

UNDERSTANDING THE NERVOUS SYSTEM was, for me, a foundational part of healing from trauma. Often, individuals who have had overwhelming and dangerous experiences find themselves stuck in shame over the way that their body responded in the scariest moments of their lives. They wonder why they couldn't speak up or run away, why they seemed unable to move, why they went along with someone, or why despite wanting to fight they stood still. We believe that if we can figure out where we went wrong, then we can keep it from happening again. It feels easier to figure out what we can fix than to acknowledge how bad it truly was.

I remember the day that the nervous system information clicked for me. Nothing special was going on, but in a matter of moments tears began streaming down my face as I realized how brilliant my body and nervous system were and how fiercely they protected me. I felt so grateful that because of all the times my nervous system fought, fled, fawned, or froze, I was alive today. Understanding that my nervous system did *exactly* what it was created to do to keep me alive—and that it continues to keep me alive—is something I am beyond grateful for.

My hope is that you can begin to understand trauma and the nervous system as it relates to your story, your healing, and your journey. Perhaps you can use this information to better understand your responses as a child. Maybe this information will help you recognize, like I did, how brilliant your nervous system is and how it kept you alive in the face of great danger. It's possible that this information will allow you to grow in compassion toward others and yourself, to decrease the shame you may feel, and to consider that your body and your nervous system have been doing an excellent job at keeping you alive.

5

Rebuilding Your Identity after the Old One No Longer Fits

I LEARNED EARLY ON IN LIFE that if I engaged in sexual activity outside of a lifelong, legal, heterosexual marriage with a cisgender man, there would be consequences. On the mild side, I could expect to feel guilt and shame. On the more extreme side, I would ruin my marriage—that is, if anyone would even consider me a suitable candidate to be a godly wife. I was terrified by these consequences, so as an adolescent I made the promise to not kiss until my wedding day.

Along with that promise, I shut down all sexual desire and arousal. Though I would still get butterflies in my stomach when I was interested in someone or when they were interested in me, I trained myself to believe that this was sinful and was often disgusted by this physiological response. As a young adult I repeatedly read the "love story" of the missionary couple Jim and Elisabeth

Elliot, hoping that my future husband and I would be like them: only attracted to how they lived out their faith in Christ.

When I began attending a progressive Southern Baptist church, I started asking questions about some of the rules around sex, modesty, and relationships. I also began dating someone. In the beginning, we spent hours mulling over these questions. For the first time in my life, my questions were welcomed and explored instead of shut down. I also began noticing different sensations in my body and had no idea that what I was experiencing was sexual arousal. Purity culture provided no education about what happens in your body when you are aroused. Even still, I welcomed these new sensations and began intentionally thinking about what a new list of sexual "dos and don'ts" might be. Before I could come up with a new list, however, my boyfriend and I began exploring our physical attraction for each other.

One Saturday evening my boyfriend came over and when I answered the door, he gently pushed me up against the wall and started kissing me. To this day, I still consider it the best first kiss I've had; it was like a rom-com, and I smile as I think about my younger self experiencing such pleasure and delight. We made our way to my bedroom, and by the end of the night I knew that I had engaged in a host of activities that I previously said would be saved for my husband. I expected to feel doubt, guilt, or fear, but I felt empowered and strong instead. I had always been told that being naked in front of a man would bring great shame, but all I felt was confidence.

I figured that this feeling wouldn't last long, that on waking the next morning I would feel heavy and dirty. But the next day when my feet touched the ground, I felt connected to myself, to God, and to the universe. To this day the only word I can use to describe the feeling is "sunshine." This struck me as odd though because it went against everything I had been taught. It was a Sunday morning, so I figured that by the time I sat through church, God would convict me. To my surprise, I felt no sense of conviction at church or at my small group that night or for weeks after, despite *begging* God to convict me.

While at a friend's house weeks later, I shared what happened as she listened with much compassion. When I finally took a breath, she asked me if I thought that I was being honest with God—that I would do whatever was necessary to repent of the sins I thought I committed. I nodded my head and exclaimed, "Yes!" She looked at me intently and said, "Then maybe you shouldn't create guilt where there isn't any." I sat back, stunned, feeling relief descend on me.

The Beginning of the Journey

Many of the people I see in clinical work sense that the worldview and identity they formed in an HCR no longer fits. Many survivors of AREs want to build a new identity. Examining one's belief system and figuring out what stays and what no longer fits— what some call deconstruction and reconstruction—goes much deeper than making cognitive shifts. As you read this book you may recognize that many of the markers of healing are connected. When we begin healing one thing, other changes follow naturally— sometimes even without having to spend concerted time, energy, or effort on them. For instance, in the story above, my engagement with sexual activity and the unexpected lack of guilt, shame, and conviction prompted me to deconstruct and reconstruct my views around sex and to heal in other ways.

In her groundbreaking work on shattered assumptions theory, researcher Ronnie Janoff-Bulman recognized that when an individual experiences extreme events or trauma, their assumptions about the world are undermined, even shattered.[1] Many people begin with assumptions that the world is a just, benevolent, and

---

1. Ronnie Janoff-Bulman, *Shattered Assumptions: Towards a New Psychology of Trauma* (New York: Free Press, 1992).

predictable place. In such a world, individuals believe they are competent, worthy, and invulnerable. Despite many HCRs teaching humans' inherent unworthiness, this theory still stands. In a backward way, believing in humans' unworthiness still feels just, benevolent, and predictable due to correlating beliefs about God's grace, love, and justice. Though one is worthy and competent only because of Jesus's death on the cross, which paved the way for God's forgiveness, the illusion of being invulnerable—namely because of God's love in Jesus Christ—remains.

When we experience overwhelming, dangerous, or scary things, including trauma, we may have trouble integrating these experiences into our worldview. Oftentimes we are left feeling defenseless, terrified, vulnerable, and confused. That's because what has happened doesn't fit the binary thinking we have been taught by an HCR. Binary thinking, also called dualistic thinking, is the belief that something exists only in opposite terms rather than on a spectrum. Something is right or wrong or good or bad. Complex problems and issues are oversimplified into being either/or. While this often provides an illusion of safety, this type of thinking does not leave room for humanity, nuance, complexity, abstract thought, objectivity, or difference.

Binary thinking works well in HCRs because it creates rules regarding what is in or out, good or bad, or right or wrong. If you are doing what is in, good, or right, you are not at risk of losing your place in the community. Though the prescription of how to live may feel rigid and stifling, because humans are wired to seek safety and security, binary thinking and living can increase the control that authorities have in a person's life. When we can recognize that following rules with the promised rewards of group inclusion and eternity in heaven fulfill our human needs for safety and connection, we can also see why an HCR is attractive.

People do not leave HCRs simply because they are bored or because they disagree with one thing. Many of the people leaving these groups were some of the most committed and devoted individuals and have painstakingly reached conclusions that led them out of their church, denomination, or faith entirely. Worldview shattering can lead to many trauma symptoms, especially when the worldview is shattered due to a traumatic or adverse experience. If someone identifies themselves exclusively or nearly exclusively by the culture or group they are part of and then their basic assumptions about this worldview or identity are shattered, then they may experience identity confusion, they may feel betrayed, and others in the group might grow suspicious of them.

As we begin to question and rebuild our worldview, we may feel shock, horror, disgust, fear, or confusion. How we feel in these moments lets us know what is happening inside us. We might notice that our heart rate increases, we feel irritable, or we feel like we could yell. These are all normal responses to our nervous system doing its job, and these feelings give us insight into feelings we may have had when the original experiences happened.

Cognitive Deconstruction

"Deconstruction" is a buzzword in contemporary conversations about religion, but its meaning can differ from person to person. For a simple illustration, we might think of a burrito bowl: we pay attention to and observe all the ingredients that go into making the burrito bowl as they are set before us individually, rather than mixed together in a burrito. This allows us to take out what we don't want and mix together what we do. Deconstructing a religious identity is something like this. In this process we examine beliefs, actions, and relationships; we consider how these shaped us and what works and does not work for us anymore. Making meaning, cognitively understanding what happened, understanding power dynamics, and even knowing how trauma lives in the body are all important for healing.

I have met with many people who have deconstructed their worldview and identity. Many would say they are happier on the other side. But I also hear the grief in their voices and see the pain on their faces. Many of them tell me that if they had known how difficult it was going to be, they may not have started. Others can hold space for both the liberation they feel in their new life as well as a deep sadness for what they lost. Still others have a lot of anger or shame, confusion, and even trepidation for what they will find when they open certain doors to their past and begin to examine those belief systems. People at the beginning stages of deconstruction have no idea how much more work is before them; many people further along stand in awe of the amazing shifts and changes they have made.

Consider some of these excerpts from the data that I collected for my dissertation:

- "I feel like I am thawing. . . . My cognitive and conscious mind have known things for months and years, but my body and subconscious mind are just catching up . . . melting . . . as if I've been frozen for years and now I can wiggle around again. . . . I am finally able to understand the atrociousness of what happened to me at the hands of others as well as how I was set up for it all along."

- "There is this overwhelming feeling of being so strong— and not even realizing how strong and amazing I was/am until now, . . . for all that I have gone through and all of the work I have done."

- "I knew that I was ready for a change—my body was telling me in no uncertain terms. I was in survival mode and as much as I could understand, my world was falling apart. But it wasn't until later that I realized how quickly it all shattered. Sitting with my therapist in the first few sessions allowed for a little crack in the walls, and then the entire wall and foundation absolutely crumbled. Literally nothing that had been real was real anymore—everything was ripped away. . . . There was a complete loss of identity, and everything I stood for was utterly chaotic. My body was so deeply indoctrinated/brainwashed that it believed that harmful things were helpful and that helpful things were harmful—doing the hard work of healing made things collapse even more. It seems like when I was finally being honest about what was happening things only got worse. *Way* worse."

These excerpts recognize that deconstructing and rebuilding a sense of identity and worldview is a process. People in this process often feel like they are both healing and have a long way to go. A marker of healing from religious trauma is not simply the process of deconstructing one's worldview and identity and rebuilding a new one; it is also the willingness to remain open to shifting and changing over the course of one's life. It is seeking growth and understanding, holding things with an open hand.

Deconstruction and Neuroscience

I admire the tenacity with which so many people have approached this deconstruction process despite having little access to professional help. Many people quickly learn that they must dig deep to fully understand what has happened and how ingrained the messages of HCRs truly are.

To understand this better, a brief lesson in neuroscience is necessary. Our brains have information messengers called neurons that use electrical impulses and chemical signals to send information back and forth between different areas of the brain *and* between the brain and the nervous system (remember, the nervous system sends messages between the brain and the body). Neurons are responsible for receiving information, also called sensory input, from the outside world and determining what to do with it. Our neurons take in this information and communicate with other parts of the brain and nervous system to determine if we are safe or in danger. When similar messages come in repeatedly or in an overwhelming fashion, the neurons create neuropathways, which over time become well-worn grooves in our brain. These neuropathways begin to function automatically and subconsciously. If something happens to us repeatedly that our brain registers as dangerous, then neurons create a pathway to immediately tell our nervous system and the other parts of our brain that danger is upon us and that something needs to be done.

Our neuropathways continue to affect how we feel even after we've cognitively rejected specific beliefs. For example, growing up in church you might have heard that you are sinful and unworthy and that feeling guilty shows that you are faithful. Later, you might reexamine that theological belief and recognize cognitively that it is wrong. You might shift to the belief that you are inherently good instead. Whew, what a relief! However, one day you do something that was at one time considered a sin, and suddenly your body feels the way it did when you were sitting in church: guilty, ashamed, and convicted. You might wonder why this is happening, since you don't hold the same beliefs anymore.

Or perhaps you grew up learning that certain people were dangerous because of their gender, sexuality, religion, social status, or the color of their skin. You may later reject labeling others in this way but still notice that when you are around a certain person, your body tenses up, your speech quickens, your face changes, or you start to get defensive. These bodily responses may surprise you; though you are not consciously frightened by this person, your body and nervous system are telling you a different story. Along with these physical responses, you may feel added suspicion, hypervigilance, and a susceptibility to creating a story about that person that matches the state of your nervous system.

These responses are happening because the old neuropathways are turning back on. Contrary to what many therapists and pseudo-therapists say online, our brains do not unlearn beliefs and concepts. But we can be intentional about creating new neuropathways. Our brains operate like this: the more a neuron fires with another neuron to create a pathway (e.g., the thought "This type of person is different from me and therefore dangerous"), the more likely it is that we will automatically have an embodied, chemical response supporting that belief. When we are conscious and intentional about creating new neuropathways, those old pathways become weaker and therefore less likely to turn on.

One final note on this concept: If, on the one hand, we stick with the definition of healing as a fixed point, then if we have one of these old, automatic reactions, it means that we haven't healed. If, on the other hand, we recognize healing as an ongoing and dynamic process, then in these bizarre moments we can notice what is happening and course correct.

This is where the practice of curiosity may be helpful. Our brain and nervous system operate under the premise that something new is unnatural. This is why we often resist new habits and patterns—our brain and body deem them unfamiliar. When someone is traumatized, they might feel activated by something new. Curiosity is an invitation out of our old patterns, habits, and familiar thoughts and behaviors. If we notice resistance toward new people, beliefs, actions, or thoughts, we can become curious about that resistance. I've adopted a simple question that researcher and author Brené Brown frequently asks her audiences to consider: "What is the story I'm telling myself?" When we can explore, without judgment toward ourselves or others, we are practicing curiosity. These questions can also show curiosity: What else could be true? What would I see if I took a different perspective? and What if my experience/perspective isn't the only one? Practicing curiosity flies in the face of fundamentalist, binary thinking because it recognizes that multiple realities can exist. Rebuilding your identity and worldview while practicing curiosity allows for continual openness and growth that lasts beyond the moment, has no fixed end point, and sidesteps shame.

Some might think that to be healed from religious trauma one must be done deconstructing previous beliefs and have built a new, firm belief system or identity. The problem is that this view can easily lead to fundamentalism—just with a different set of beliefs. Rebuilding a worldview and identity likely needs to include space for uncertainty. Though humans thrive on stability, we may need to consider whether in constructing a new belief system and identity we are, once again, relying on external resources, beliefs, and practices to give us stability and safety rather than tapping into our own internal resources and inherent goodness.

Embodied Fundamentalism

While deconstruction is often a necessary starting point in moving out of HCRs, it is not the same as healing from religious trauma. The cognitive knowledge of what has happened is often extremely helpful, even foundational, for people. However, this knowledge is not the same as understanding how those beliefs have been ingrained in your mind and body. This is why so many people feel confused when, for example, after rejecting purity-culture beliefs, they still feel a great amount of guilt, shame, and even physical pain when engaging in consensual sexual activity. It's one thing to point out and cognitively reject purity culture beliefs; it's a different process to understand how these beliefs live inside your body months and years after you have mentally left them behind.

This sense of embodied fundamentalism is often the reason some people jump from one fundamentalist system to another. Religion certainly has not cornered the market on fundamentalism; many other groups and systems are fundamentalist despite no religious affiliation. Fundamentalism is a pattern of thinking and relating; it is the belief that a certain person or group of people know the right way to think, act, talk, relate, believe, and engage with the world *and* that those who do not subscribe to this worldview are lesser than, dangerous, pitied, hard to relate to, or to be avoided. We often see this in various wellness communities, multilevel marketing companies, cults, social media, and lifestyle groups.

I believe fundamentalism is a coping mechanism to deal with a dysregulated nervous system. As we saw in chapter 4, we know that humans thrive on what is familiar. This is why people and ideas that are different may seem dangerous and why an overactive SNS triggers a fight or flight response. In those moments our nervous system is trying to figure out what will help us calm down and feel safe again. Fundamentalism helps with that: it gives specific, orderly, binary, prescriptive ways of engaging with life. It's a measuring stick that lets you know how you are doing and what you can do more (or less) of to remain in good standing and, therefore, safe and stable. Doing or thinking what the specific fundamentalist group prescribes can give you a sense of peace and reassure you that you are not in danger because you are doing what you are supposed to be doing.

For the individual who has grown up in a system like this, the cognitive idea of being free and being able to live how they want might sound liberating. But the lived experience can feel disarming and destabilizing. As I was leaving fundamentalism, I replaced many of my spiritual practices and beliefs with different wellness and dietary regimens that were meant to get me to the place of healing that I desired. For others this might look like adopting new ideologies, practices, or groups. This too can be useful to reflect on. Are there areas of your life where fundamentalist thinking or relating still exists? Perhaps you have beliefs, practices, or ways of relating that are difficult to move out of. Or perhaps when others engage differently you rush to make assumptions, judge others, or defend yourself. What might it look like to practice curiosity instead?

Part of rebuilding your worldview and identity may include taking stock of how fundamentalism lives inside you—how you may be a fundamentalist even if you have left religion. HCRs determine which voices are worth listening to. This is often based on gender, age, experience, and platform. Sometimes we carry these biases into other realms of our lives and gravitate toward the same type of people that we did while in the religious environment.

For example, those of us coming out of HCRs are often trained to listen to the voices of white men as spiritual authorities. As we forge new identities, the voices of white men may still be most appealing, since those are the voices we're used to trusting. On social media, many accounts that gain followers quickly are almost exclusively white or white-passing men. A quick glance through posts on various social media platforms reveals that many people have left an HCR but are still living, thinking, and relating to others from a place of embodied fundamentalism. We should exercise caution and employ curiosity regarding who we listen to on social media. Notice if the voices you are most prone to listening to resemble the same types of people you looked and listened to while in an HCR. Observe whether you gravitate toward people and accounts that offer prescriptions and answers that worked for them and are now being touted as the keys to healing or being truly deconstructed. Though large accounts and loud voices appeal to those of us coming out of HCRs, the appeal may be based on the familiarity of being told what to do, think, and how to act instead of promoting autonomy, choice, and freedom.

An appeal of fundamentalism is the illusion of certainty that it offers; fundamentalism prescribes what is right, good, and true and encourages people to discard critical thinking and curiosity. This means that when new or unfamiliar situations arise, fundamentalist teachings and thinking feel like soft landing pads as they offer concrete answers and steps for how to do things the right way. For instance, I have many clients who have done a lot of work related to the purity culture messages they heard growing up. Many have developed an entirely new sexual ethic for themselves, and yet when it comes to helping their children develop a sexual ethic, they struggle to not revert to old teachings, ways of thinking, and rules. This is because they have entered unknown territory, and that feels scary. When we feel scared, it's easy to revert to old ways of thinking and relating that feel familiar and safer. Fundamentalism is a well-worn groove that is easy to step back into.

The Importance of Choice

A few days after I moved to the South, I was writing in my journal and had an aha moment: I could be whoever I wanted. The thought was exciting and terrifying. It is a gift and privilege to be able to start over. While I knew that I wanted to change a lot from my previous life, when push came to shove it felt too scary and too overwhelming to do it all at once. Realistically, I could take only little steps. However, those little, manageable steps eventually took me quite a distance from where I started.

One of the foundational parts of rebuilding a new worldview and identity is *choice*. In your previous life someone was prescribing life choices for you. They told you who you were, what to do, what to believe, how to dress, how to act, how every moment of your life should be spent. They dictated your entire identity. Sometimes when we get out of HCRs we swing to the other side of the spectrum. Never having had the opportunity to make our own choices means that often the only "choice" is to do the exact opposite of what we were taught or how we lived before. However, this pendulum swing is not really characterized by choice either. Sure, it might be more fun and feel freer, but if we are merely doing the opposite of what we have previously done, that too is prescribed.

True choice involves thought, intention, and curiosity, allowing you to make the decision that is most in line with who you are and what you value. To be sure, sometimes we need to go to other extremes so that we have a gauge from which to make choices. Perhaps being able to make choices will take us beyond prescribed ways of living. Choice means you may keep some things from your old life in addition to discarding a lot of stuff. Regardless of the choices you make, you'll be able to make them freely and base them on what you value.

The Beginning of Healing

You might be asking yourself, "So where is the healing in this?"

For many people, the beginning of deconstructing a worldview and an identity can feel all-consuming. This is usually because they are being flooded with information and seeing, often for the first time, how many things no longer add up. Their brain is swimming with new information; their world may feel shattered. If that is where you are right now, keep up the hard work. It does get better. For others who have already gone through stages like this, congratulations! You might notice that while areas to deconstruct do keep coming up, they don't come at the same pace or with the same intensity they once had. Perhaps they don't feel as daunting either. Some of you may be decades into this process, and deconstruction hardly crosses your mind in a conscious way anymore; you notice when things surface from the past, and sometimes you can even chuckle at the absurdity of something or give yourself a pat on the back for how far you have come. To you I say, well done!

Regardless of where you are, remember that this is your process and each step you take is a step of healing. It can feel tempting to listen to certain loud voices on social media platforms, on the internet, in books, and on podcasts who say you *must* deconstruct certain topics or that you *must* land at a certain place or that to *truly* be deconstructed you must also make certain other changes. But this process is about choice, and you get to make many of them. There will be awkward or uncomfortable moments, but when those moments arise because you are desiring to live from your values, then even the uncomfortable, difficult stuff can be rewarding.

Finally, be patient with yourself. It's okay to take breaks. Many of us are upending everything we thought was true about ourselves and the world. This is no small task; in fact, it takes an incredibly brave person.

And if I may: give yourself many moments to reflect on how far you have come, how many steps you have taken, and how different you are. Each step that you take, each time you catch yourself going back into old thought or behavior patterns, and each time you sense in your body old feelings and sensations that no longer match what you believe now is a moment of healing. These are all moments where you can see and feel and live the change. Give yourself a pat on the back—you deserve it.

6

Engaging in a Relationship with Your Body

WHEN I WAS NINETEEN YEARS OLD, I did my first forty-day, liquids-only fast during Lent. I was taught that Lent was a time to focus on my relationship with God. I grew up in the era of Gwen Shamblin's Weigh Down workshops, where I learned that being fat was a sin, that I idolized food, and that God should be my sustenance. So I embarked on this fast to show God how committed I was to him. I earnestly believed that if Jesus could do this, as evidenced by biblical accounts of Jesus fasting, then I could too. I knew I would be tempted by food, and I reasoned that if I could withstand this temptation, my faith would be stronger.

With permission from my parents and our evangelical family physician, I embarked on this task every year, at least once a year, for over a decade.

On the outside, my fasting appeared impressive. Though I never made a show of fasting, it was hard to disguise. I couldn't exercise for very long, would become more irritable, and had noticeable physical changes. I chalked up particular sensations in my body to the Holy Spirit working through me. I now know that I was starving my body through a severe calorie deficit and was in a constant state of SNS activation. As I ignored my body's pleas for sustenance, I believed that I was honoring God. I always felt a sense of sadness when the Lent season came to an end, because I would then have to struggle with the sins of craving food over God or of eating food to sustain myself rather than depending on God to meet my every need.

The concept of making my body a slave to Christ was appealing. I experienced comfort and felt safe believing that someone else was in control of my life. Hating my body was a natural extension of this. Purity culture taught me that my body was evil because of the temptation it posed to men, while fundamentalism taught me that my body was evil because I was born totally depraved. Next to my need for a savior, not trusting myself, which ultimately included vilifying my body, was a close second in the rank of important teachings. Expressing my emotions, listening to my bodily sensations, or moving my body in certain ways were met with critique and shame. This often meant that I needed to override cues for being hungry or full, ignore the way I felt, and scrutinize the way I walked, stood, and moved my body so as not to cause others to stumble into sin.

As I began resolving my religious trauma, I had to pay attention to my body in a new way. My last attempt at a forty-day fast was unsuccessful. I made it to day twenty-one and finally heard my body screaming, "Stop!" I had known my body was signaling this before, but for the first time I was listening.

Messages about the Body in High-Control Religions

Writing about her own experience with evangelicalism, Jamie Lee Finch described what it felt like to believe she was inherently flawed and evil: "For most of my life I believed my own body was dangerous. This belief caused me to subconsciously turn her into my own enemy and she assumed the role and acted the part."[1]

When we repeatedly hear negative messages about our own or others' bodies, we internalize these beliefs in our bodies. Words from the pulpit or from influential leaders—including parents, partners, or the surrounding culture—about who we are or how our bodies affect others are taught as absolute. The choice to not accept such teachings about the body are met with harsh consequence that may threaten one's place within the group. Thus, not only do we cognitively accept negative and dangerous views of our bodies, but we internalize these views so much that we act the roles we are given. As I was writing this chapter, I posted a question to my Instagram story asking my followers what their religion taught them about their or others' bodies that had caused harm, distrust, shame, or confusion. I received hundreds of answers. Here are some examples:

- If you're immodest and cause boys to lust, you're responsible.
- The heart is deceitful and wicked; who can know it?
- My flesh is evil; I cannot trust myself at all.
- I should listen to authority rather than to myself.
- God gets to use my body however and whenever he wants.
- Every single piece of me is hated by God because of original sin.
- Having a larger body is the result of serving food over God and is therefore idolatry.
- I am not healed from physical illness because I have unconfessed sin or unforgiveness in my heart.
- Bodies are a direct reflection of morality; a thin and self-controlled person is godly.

1. Jamie Lee Finch, *You Are Your Own: A Reckoning with the Religious Trauma of Evangelical Christianity* (self-published, 2019), 53.

- There is an ideal body that means a woman is holy: white, thin, able-bodied.
- Touching of genitals was considered so bad that I didn't properly wash them in the shower/bath for years.
- My body is separate from me, was wicked, and could not be trusted.
- "The flesh is weak"; therefore, I cannot trust my body's intuitions and needs.

I noticed that nearly every response had something to do with one of two themes: bodies and sexuality or sexual expression and others' experiences of our bodies. Here are some examples:

- My body was responsible for my sexual assault.
- My body is an object for men.
- Dressing my body in a certain way is a distraction to men and an invitation for them to sexualize me. Even sexual assault would be my fault.
- I had to neurotically monitor my every movement—even touching my hair could turn a man on.
- If I don't take care of my body through not exercising or overeating, I am not honoring God or my husband—this also makes it more likely that my husband might cheat on me, and it would be at least partially my fault.
- Self-pleasure is considered sinful, and therefore I was delayed in learning about my own body's needs and pleasures.
- My body, specifically my long legs, were a problem with no solution. My problem would tempt men, but it was also so difficult to hide my legs!

In many HCRs, the body and sexuality are synonymous. While it is true that our sexuality, sexual expression, and body are inextricably linked, these are also distinct. One's body should not be reduced to its sexual purposes. In a podcast interview, Nadia Bolz-Weber was asked why she believed religion was so focused on rules around sex. The interviewer was confused as to why so many religions create rigid rules around people's sexuality and bodies and why they seem obsessed with controlling bodies, sexuality, and sexual expression. Her answer, paraphrased, was that the church views sex as its competition.

One of the most effective ways an HCR can gain control over people is by creating a narrative around the body that promotes shame, sinfulness, and an external locus of control, meaning that a person cannot trust themselves or their body. This narrative is often constructed in both overt and covert ways. Many fundamentalist religions teach that a human is evil and sinful from the time they are born and that they have no ability to choose what is good or right apart from God's saving grace. A message like this lays a foundation of distrust; people can't trust themselves because of how sinful they are. Additionally, a high value is placed on a religious leader's words, meaning that the rules they make are seen as God's rules. Questioning these rules could be seen as an act of rebellion or sinfulness that a person would need to repent from. Many people have grown up in systems like this, and thus it may feel impossible for them to see their body as anything but evil.

I distinctly remember one message I received about my body when I was young. I was five years old, sitting on the hump of the wheel well in the back of my dad's truck with the neighbor boy who was a year older. As my dad cleaned the truck, I rested my head on the neighbor boy's shoulder, and he leaned his head in and rested his head on mine. In that instant my body came alive. I felt like I had unlocked the keys to the universe. I vividly remember thinking that *this* is what life was about and that I never wanted it to end. I was so mesmerized by how my body felt that I hardly noticed my dad tapping my shoulder; he finally tapped so hard that I had to come out of my fantasy world and face him. He told me to get inside the house.

Later that evening my parents sat me down to let me know how inappropriately I had acted. I couldn't understand what I had done wrong, so I assumed that everything about the situation was wrong—how I had felt, what my body had done, how alive I had become, and this fantasy world that I wanted to live in. My parents had told me it was wrong, which meant that if I did it again, I would be disobeying them.

Ten years later, in the thick of purity culture, I put that experience into the category of "awakening love before it was time." Experiences like these may seem silly to those outside HCRs; they may even seem silly or benign to our adult selves, but these moments taught many of us that sexuality was sinful and so were our bodies.

In chapter 1, I mentioned my experience with dissociation and discussed findings from trauma research suggesting that individuals who experience religious trauma often learn how to dissociate (to leave their bodies to protect themselves from a real or perceived threat).[2] This is called disembodiment. An individual coming out of an HCR might not only feel that their body is dangerous but also celebrate the idea of dissociation. When an individual is disembodied, they're no longer attuned to internal body cues, and their sense of self and time is altered. For individuals with religious trauma, this means that becoming embodied is not only essential for trauma resolution and recovery but also a direct act of defiance against the religious power and control that was wielded against them.

Talking about being in your body may sound well and good, but the actual experience of it is often much more difficult. It's often a slow process of taking two steps forward and one step

---

2. Judith Herman, *Trauma and Recovery: The Aftermath of Violence—From Domestic Abuse to Political Terror* (New York: Basic Books, 1992).

back, as an individual carefully learns how to navigate a new relationship to their body. For many of us the mere idea that we have a body and that it is ours can feel wildly uncomfortable. And yet, in healing from trauma, the body is truly where the work needs to happen.

Developing a New Relationship with Your Body

In the previous chapter I discussed making cognitive shifts and deconstructing worldviews and beliefs that no longer work, as well as rebuilding a new framework from which to live. However, if we stop there, even though we might be able to think well or even preach a different message to ourselves and the people around us, we are often still subject to the messages and practices of HCRs living within us.

I often use this analogy with my clients: Imagine that you have an acquaintance—someone you've known your entire life—whom you despise. You tolerate them, but you generally disdain them. When they show up, you say mean things about them, telling them how much you hate them and how much you wish they would change. You might even call them names or call them out for their flaws. Then one day you realize that this acquaintance of yours is a good person! They have been there for you even when you have been cruel to them. They've even advocated for you, despite how much you complain about their presence. You turn and look at this person with newfound admiration and respect. You tell them that you've changed, that they should trust you, and that what you want for them is for their own good. Understandably, this person would be cautious and probably not too sure they should believe you. It would rightfully take them time and demand consistency on your part—probably a lot of it—to learn to trust that you have truly changed and that you want to engage in a mutually loving and respectful relationship with them.

What if this acquaintance is your body?

HCRs disconnect us from our bodies. So does trauma. The combination of the two often makes our bodies scary or undesirable places to be. Moreover, living inside our bodies in HCRs and when experiencing trauma often feels like too much to bear, so we dissociate, suppress, stifle, shut down, and numb. We call our bodies disgusting and vile, beat them up, starve them, pinch them, pull them, contort them, and sometimes harm them; they learn that even though they must stick around, they are not welcome or wanted. So when we wake up and discover the deep damage of HCRs and the trauma we've experienced, it takes more than the epiphany to move from hating our bodies to loving them.

To demonstrate how the cognitive messages about our bodies *live* in our bodies, I am going to invite you to do an exercise. This activity encourages you to tune into your body and notice sensations. For some people this will feel difficult, uncomfortable, or even intolerable. Please do what is best for you. There is no right way to think or feel as you are doing this activity. It's all about you and noticing your automatic responses and sensations.

If it feels okay, take a moment, gaze down at your body, and say, "This is my body." When you say that, what do you notice? Perhaps you feel resistance or disgust. Maybe your chest opens or tightens, your cheeks flush or your face gets hot, your heart starts beating faster or a smile creeps onto your face. It's possible you feel a sense of heaviness, cold, or numbness. Or maybe you feel relief, you sigh, or you feel rooted to the ground.

If it feels okay, let's up the ante a bit. (Again, you do not need to do this activity if you do not feel safe or comfortable to do so!) Say, "I love my body." Notice what happens. Perhaps some of the same feelings or sensations come up for you that I described in the prior paragraph. Or maybe you feel something different. Perhaps this statement, as you say it, feels untrue, and you feel resistance somewhere in your body. Simply notice that. Notice where your thoughts go: Do you start scanning your body for flaws? Do you think back to the ways you are imperfect or messages that you were told? Is your mind flooded with words from spiritual leaders about how loving your body is idolatry?

The purpose of this brief exercise is to help you understand how your brain and body operate together to take in and believe new messages. Healing from trauma is about giving your body a different experience than what it has been allowed to have during a real or perceived threat. Therefore, for many people, saying "I love my body" or even "This is my body" can feel cognitively believable, since you've changed your viewpoints on the body, while still feeling untrue in your body's experience.

What Is Embodiment?

Embodiment is a daily, moment-by-moment practice that is both grueling and rewarding. Embodiment does not guarantee positive or pleasant experiences all the time—instead it means that you feel everything, you live everything, and you move through everything.

According to therapists Hillary McBride and Janelle Kwee, the term "embodiment" refers to the experience of living *as* a body while engaging with the world. In addition, they identify embodiment as both a solitary, individual, and internal experience of the body and as an experience shaped by external factors—namely, social discourse and relationships.[3] In his research, Max van Manen refers to the use of one's body as a way of knowing; this kind of knowledge "resides in our actions, situations, relations, and of course our bodies."[4] Embodiment allows an individual to know themselves, to relate to others, and to experience the world by tapping into the feelings that exist within their body, allowing then to sense, to communicate nonverbally, and to receive communication. McBride and Kwee suggest that through

3. Hillary L. McBride and Janelle L. Kwee, *Embodiment and Eating Disorders: Theory, Research, Prevention, and Treatment* (New York: Routledge, 2018).

4. Max van Manen, *Phenomenology of Practice: Meaning-Giving Methods in Phenomenological Research and Writing* (New York: Routledge, 2014), 270.

the embodied experience—that is, experiencing life through the body—we can "most readily know life and all of its pleasure, pain, and feelings."[5]

These three researchers acknowledge that embodiment is not prioritized in our culture. They note that individuals are often unaware of their bodies unless or until they are in pain, uncomfortable, or ill. This often leads to a disembodied self—meaning that a person either represses feelings, silences them, or dissociates. In Judith Herman's research on trauma and the body, she notes that when an individual undergoes extreme, severe, and/or prolonged traumatic experiences, it is common for them to leave their body—that is, dissociate—to protect themselves from real or perceived threat.[6] Others echo Herman's work by noting that disembodiment is often the result of extreme trauma, which can alter an individual's sense of self and time along with their ability to remain present and attuned to internal bodily cues.[7]

Moving from *having* a body to *being* a body is an important part of embodiment and healing. McBride writes, "Being a body, seeing the self as inextricable from our physicality and our physicality as the expression of our personhood, invites us into wholeness. But when the self has been shattered and fragmented—as it has been for many of us—collecting the fragments, believing they belong to us, and naming them as good is a politically rebellious, spiritually powerful, and biomedically healing practice."[8] Later in her book, McBride suggests that embodiment is the practice of recognizing that our bodies are not distinct from our minds and ourselves. Simply put, *I am my body.*

5. McBride and Kwee, *Embodiment and Eating Disorders*, 11.

6. Herman, *Trauma and Recovery*.

7. Laura E. Anderson, "The Living Experience of Healing the Sexually Traumatized Self" (PhD diss., Saybrook University, 2021), ProQuest (No. 28644488); Angela Connolly, "Abject Bodies: Trauma, Shame, Disembodiment and the Death of Time," in *Temporality and Shame: Perspectives from Psychoanalysis and Philosophy*, ed. Ladson Hinton and Hessel Willemsen (London: Routledge, 2017), 101–18.

8. Hillary L. McBride, *The Wisdom of Your Body: Finding Healing, Wholeness, and Connection through Embodied Living* (Grand Rapids: Brazos, 2021), 15.

Embodiment is a practice and a commitment. Our bodies hear everything we have said and see everything we have done and, therefore, need new experiences to know that it is safe to be in this world. Just like another human would likely not dive into a relationship with someone who has been cruel and cold to them for decades, our bodies also need time to learn that we are no longer engaging in the thoughts and behaviors that require us to silence, enslave, and harm them.

Think for a moment about the process of befriending someone or beginning to date someone. How do you act during this process? Do you remain quiet and aloof? Or do you engage in conversation and express curiosity? Do you make time for the other person and practice intentionality, or do you leave things to chance?

When I introduce this concept to my clients, they often groan and roll their eyes. I chuckle because I get it. It would be much easier if our bodies would believe that, despite calling them names yesterday, they should engage in a mutually beneficial relationship today.

There are many ways to begin engaging in a relationship with your body. For some people it helps to shift the language they use to refer to their body—for example, calling their body by a pronoun instead of referring to their body as "it." Other people commit to listening to their body's natural cues for hunger, sleep, and elimination. There is not one right way to become embodied or to move from hatred to love, and whatever way you choose will take time and patience. Just like in human-to-human relationships, where we need time to get to know someone before we trust them or experience intimacy with them, it will take our bodies time to soften into this new way of moving through the world.

The following excerpt extrapolated from related research aptly describes what it is like to enter this new relationship with your body. As you read it, notice how this response contrasts with the responses to my Instagram post earlier in this chapter.

I do believe my body is always working for my greatest good. My body does not lie. But I also realize my body works for my survival—which means that sometimes my body does things that cognitively do not make sense because she believes that is what is best—in order to protect me. . . .

My body was told for so long how sinful and disgusting she was and how I needed to, essentially, kill her off that maybe she just began to believe it. But now, I hate the evidence of the trauma; I do not hate my body. I hate the evidence of the trauma on my body. My weight gain has been the result of trauma after trauma after trauma with no treatment, just stuffing down my feelings as hard as I could and then trying to kill them off.

Now, I must trust this process: that my body intuitively knows how to heal. My responsibility is to create the space and safety to allow her to express and trust her to do what she already knows how to do.

I still get teary when I read that. Whereas HCRs seek to separate a person from their body, embodiment builds a whole person. This is not to suggest that every whim, desire, or response our body has is 100 percent healthy, accurate, or in our best interest. As the data suggest, our bodies may be working for survival under a pretty messed up set of rules.[9] Instead, embodiment connects every part of us so that we can listen to the information our body is giving us, lovingly and intentionally respond, and walk through the world in a new way.

Earlier in this chapter I proposed relating to our bodies the way we would relate to another human. The language of relationship is, for most people, a foundational way to begin practicing embodiment. Like developing a relationship with another human, developing a relationship with your body takes time, patience, and intention. When we are seeking to get to know someone, we prioritize them in our lives and schedules, we listen with intent, we express curiosity about what they are communicating, and we

9. Anderson, "Living Experience of Healing."

recognize that it takes time to get to know and trust someone. The same is true with our bodies—even more so when our relationship with our bodies has been defined by beliefs that our bodies are evil, that bodily sensations should be suppressed, and that we should ignore our bodies at every opportunity. When seeking to become embodied after leaving an HCR, you should expect that a relationship with your body may not come easily. Our bodies may not easily trust that, after years or decades of abusing, ignoring, and silencing them, we really mean it when we say we will listen and change the way we live accordingly.

For me, it took about two years of actively, daily checking in with my body, paying attention to the sensations and emotions that were arising, and using that information as guidance in how I lived before I really had a sense that my body trusted me—and that I trusted my body. It's not lost on me that this is approximately the same amount of time it takes me to truly trust another human with whom I've engaged in intentional relationship! Consider the exercise a few paragraphs above where I asked you to reflect on the relationships you have with other humans and to notice the ways you have entered and engaged in relationships. What would it be like to apply that same enthusiasm to a relationship with your body? How might you intentionally spend time with, listen to, and maintain a curious stance toward your body? What would shift in the way you speak to and about your body? How might you listen differently, and how might you shift the way you act accordingly?

Embodying New Messages

Several years ago, I stumbled across the concept of introjection. Introjection is the "unconscious adoption of the ideas or attitudes of others."[10] I understand introjection as the process that happens

---

10. Found online at Google Dictionary, https://www.google.com/search?q=introjection+definition&rlz=1C1GCEU_enUS1030US1030&oq.

when we are told by others how to think, feel, or experience and then internalize these messages so that we believe they are coming from within us. As it pertains to our bodies, this means that the messages we were told over and over—from family, friends, culture, and religion—became the messages we believed about ourselves. This is where the lessons of neuroscience from earlier in the book come in. Our brains and bodies work together in this way when we repeatedly hear the same messages or have overwhelming experiences. Our brains create neuropathways that send signals to our bodies. Our bodies then release specific chemicals and have certain responses based on the messages our brains receive. Often when a client tells me a negative message that they believe, the conversation goes like this:

> ME: Whose voice is saying that you are not worthy of love?
>
> CLIENT: Me. It's my voice.
>
> ME: So you've always had a voice inside you saying that you were not worthy of love? Is it possible that someone told you that message so frequently that you began to believe it?
>
> CLIENT: Maybe . . .
>
> ME: Let's sit for a moment with that question. "Whose voice is saying that?"
>
> CLIENT: (*Pauses.*) You know, I don't know whose voice that is, but it doesn't seem like it's mine.
>
> ME: Excellent, let's go with that. For right now, or maybe forever, we don't need to know whose voice it is, we just need to know that it's not *your* voice. All we need to know is that at some point someone, or many people, told you this so often that you believed it. You heard it so often you even believed that it was your voice.

CLIENT: Wow, . . . that's a lot! What do I do with that?

ME: Well, the first step is to recognize when that voice is speaking and start to realize that it's not your voice. Maybe you can even remind yourself of that somehow. You might catch yourself saying that you are not worthy of love, and then perhaps you could pause and say, "I don't know whose voice that is, but it's certainly not mine!" Could we try that right now?

CLIENT: We can try.

ME: Let's imagine you're making dinner tonight and that voice says, "You're not worthy of love." What next?

CLIENT: Whoa. Stop. I don't know whose voice that is, but it's not mine.

ME: That's great. Let's pause for a moment. . . . As you said that, what did you notice in your body?

CLIENT: There is a little resistance, like I'm not sure if I believe it. But there is also some curiosity, like, what if that isn't my voice?

ME: Excellent! Let's stay with that. What if? What if that isn't your voice?

CLIENT: Well, if it isn't my voice, I suppose I may not have to believe it.

ME: Could you tell that voice to shut up? What if we could say "shut up" to that voice, what would that feel like?

CLIENT: "Shut up! That's not my voice!" Whoa. That's kind of a rush!

ME: What do you notice?

CLIENT: I feel a little bit powerful!

ME: Oh, nice! Where do you feel that?

CLIENT: I feel it in my upper arms, almost like I've just
    lifted some really heavy weights and I'm flexing!

ME: That's great! If you would be okay with it, let's flex
    our arms together and say, "Shut up!" Would you
    feel comfortable with that?

CLIENT: Yes, it's fine.

BOTH OF US: (*Both flex arms.*) "Shut up!"

(*Silence follows for a few moments.*)

ME: What was that like for you?

CLIENT: I feel a little different. I don't know that I believe
    that I am worthy of love, but I also don't think I
    believe that original message as much.

We cannot think trauma away; this is why embodiment and having a loving relationship with your body is so important for trauma resolution. We need our bodies to be on board, and we need to feel safe enough in our bodies to be able to give them a new experience. If you reread the dialogue above, you'll notice that the client originally feels very close to the negative message; they even believe that it is coming from within them. It feels so true that a different message feels like a lie. However, when we slowly inch our way, with curiosity, toward a different possibility—by asking the simple question "What if that isn't your voice?"—we give ourselves the opportunity to have a tiny, but powerful, new experience in our bodies.

Negative messages still come up for me sometimes, and I am surprised they are still hanging around and rearing their ugly heads. When these messages come up, I work with them. I do this because I am no longer interested in my body believing anything that harms her. The messages that I had to believe to survive an abusive religious environment are no longer useful for me. The coping mechanisms that kept me alive at one point will now suffocate me, unless I am willing to give my body a new experience so that I can learn to embody a new truth.

AN EMBODIED LIFE—that is, a life where you recognize your body as your self—is not a life free from pain and strife. Having a relationship with your body means that you will feel pain; it means that you will feel everything. It does not mean that you must live a life of sorrow, seclusion, or constant sadness. Rather, a relationship with your body is an invitation to lean deeper into your internal experience with compassion and curiosity and to hear what your body is saying, to honor what your body needs, and to provide a new experience. As Bessel van der Kolk asserts, our bodies truly do keep the score. Our bodies hold the stories of what has happened to us, but they also hold the map to healing. Our bodies are brilliant and can lead us home, to ourselves, if we will let them.

One extraordinary benefit of developing a loving relationship with your body is the natural love and respect you gain toward others' bodies. It's a near automatic extension. When I love my body, when I humanize myself, I love and humanize others. This is an act of rebellion in HCRs. Loving your body opens space to love, understand, and have empathy and compassion for every other body, no matter how similar or different those bodies are from your own. This gives us boldness to treat each body with respect, dignity, and kindness. It allows us to stand against the oppression of marginalized bodies and empowers us to do something about it. Loving my body lets me love your body: the human in me sees the human in you, and that changes the world.

7

Stabilizing the Nervous System

ON A MILD WINTER DAY, I began walking on my favorite trail. I knew every turn, tree, and side trail; I had walked this path just the day before. Suddenly my heart rate skyrocketed, my vision tunneled, and I began to sweat profusely. Puzzled, I stopped, cupped my hands over my mouth, and tried to regulate my breathing. After a few moments my breathing slowed and, thinking the bizarre experience must have been a fluke, I began walking again. Less than a minute later my heart rate skyrocketed again, and the scene repeated itself. As I made my way down the trail, I began analyzing what had just happened, wondering if I was warding off a panic attack. I soon approached a long hill with a rather steep incline and paused, wondering if I should turn around and head back to my car.

Something inside urged me to go on, however, and fearing another panic attack, I intuitively began engaging all my senses. I felt my feet hit the ground as I took each step, I heard wind rustling through the trees, I smelled spring in the air, and I watched my dog scamper along the path beside me. As I tuned in to these senses, orienting myself to the moment, I noticed something peculiar: my heart rate began decreasing as I was walking *up* the hill. I got to the top of the hill and burst into tears. I knew that my body had just had a deep and transformative experience. I thanked my body for this and leaned in further, seeking to understand what happened.

In the coming days and weeks, I discovered that my body had been living in a constant state of activation for years. My body perceived danger in *anything* that increased my heart rate, even something that was considered healthy, like exercise. For years I had sullenly joked that my body had the opposite reaction to exercise than other people's bodies did. As I considered my experience and began to research, I realized that my seemingly nonchalant and sarcastic observation was indeed true.[1]

I walked the trail faithfully, several times each week, for months, helping my body learn how to feel safe even when my heart rate was elevated. Ten months after that initial experience, I climbed the hill again, noticing my heart rate increasing due only to the climb and not because I felt endangered. I again burst into tears at the top of the hill, thanking my body for trusting this process and for finding safety within myself.

HCRs and an Activated Nervous System

My clients and I regularly discuss social media. Despite leaving HCRs, many of them like to remain connected to people within those systems through social media. Many feel that this connection allows them to keep track of what is happening in others' lives from a safe distance. Yet as they scroll through their feeds, many of my clients feel anxious, triggered, irritable, angry, scared, and nauseous. As they see posts and photos promoting the system's

---

1. Rebecca A. Munsey, Adrian S. Warren, and H. Ray Wooten, "Body-Centered Self-Defense for Survivors of Sexual Assault," *Journal of Professional Counseling* 42, no. 2 (2015): 17–27.

messages, their physiological symptoms may increase despite them knowing that they are in the safety of their home or car.

Though many of my clients choose to unfollow, block, or mute people from their former life, it's often impossible to do so entirely. Many clients still have family members and long-standing relationships with people in the HCR, and blocking them feels overwhelming or isolating. According to Stephen W. Porges's research, my clients' bodies and nervous systems are responding to the perception of threat, even though in most cases they are safe.[2] My work with clients may include setting the aforementioned boundaries, but even then it is nearly impossible to block, unfollow, or mute every triggering message and photo. What then becomes more important is helping my client develop internalized safety and stability so that when they see or feel something that causes distress, they can regulate themselves.

HCRs thrive on highly activated nervous systems. Individuals in these systems are taught to be on guard all the time. But our SNS is meant to be engaged in short bursts. For instance, if we are being chased by a tiger, we want our nervous systems to turn on and help us (likely) flee or freeze to survive this encounter. When the threat has passed, our nervous system is designed to return to stasis. However, when our nervous system is continuously activated, our bodies become very unsafe places to be, and external environments and people are our only hope of finding safety. Therefore, following the rules and beliefs of the HCR becomes important: it's an easy measurement of whether someone is doing okay and whether they can feel safe and calm, even if only for a moment.

An activated nervous system often leads to irritability, anxiety, fear, guilt, shame, and other intense emotions. These emotions

2. Stephen W. Porges, "Making the World Safe for Our Children: Down-Regulating Defence and Up-Regulating Social Engagement to 'Optimise' the Human Experience," *Children Australia* 40, no. 2 (2015): 83–93, https://doi.org/1.00r.g1/107.171/0778/80688262065015616663366394.

are often accompanied by physiological sensations. We may feel anxiety in our belly, guilt in our chest, and the feeling of wanting to crawl out of our skin when we feel shame. In HCRs, rather than understanding these physiological responses as an over-active nervous system, they are often taken to be conviction from God. The anxiety you feel in your belly indicates that you have unconfessed sin. The guilt you feel in your chest reveals a hardened heart, that you have sinned, or that you have idolized yourself or someone or something else. Rather than viewing emotions as information that helps us understand our internal landscape, these sensations are viewed as the way the Holy Spirit convicts us, and we are once again led away from our bodies and required to outsource feelings of peace and safety.

While the state of our nervous system can sometimes feel overwhelming, it can also act as a magnifying glass to what is happening inside us. Given the ability to slow down and turn inward, we may see that what we mistook for conviction or God's voice was our body asking us to rest, telling us that something didn't feel right, or telling us that we were acting outside of our value system. These feelings can show us where we need to establish a boundary, renegotiate relationships, or ask for help. In my research, the theme of engaging with the nervous system in a new way emerged over and over, and it became clear that many HCRs have hijacked our most precious resource as a way to gain more control over individuals and the group of people in the system.

Trauma Responses and Triggers

A trauma trigger is any experience, inner sensation, emotion, sensorial factor, or environmental factor that the body and nervous system identify as similar to a previous situation that was perceived to be dangerous, overwhelming, or unsafe. When someone experiences a trigger, they often experience involuntary psychological or physiological responses because the body believes it is existing "back then"—that is, when it was in danger. Though a person may be able to consciously recognize that they are in the present moment, their nervous system has begun working for their survival. When a person is triggered, their PFC shuts down, and they begin operating from the parts of the brain that can rationalize any behavior in the service of survival, even if it's not rational. Being triggered can feel scary and confusing. For folks who have not been able to develop internal resources for coping, it can take several hours or even days to feel normal again.

It is not uncommon to have a client begin a session by telling me they are discouraged about having many triggers. Many of them quietly wonder if this means that the practices we are engaging in are not working. In most cases they tell me that they recognized what was happening and then implemented one of the skills or techniques we had been working on. They usually look at me with shock as a smile creeps onto my face and I tell them how incredibly they handled it. Healing does not mean never being triggered. Please hear me say that again: the goal of healing from trauma is not that you will never be triggered. Rather, a marker of living in a healing body after religious trauma is that *when* you are triggered, you can access different resources internally so that a different ending can occur.

Victims of sexualized violence often express confusion regarding why their body did what it did in the face of danger. They wanted to run or fight back but were unable to do so because they felt frozen. They often blame themselves for this and feel ashamed. This is true for others who face real, perceived, or remembered threat or overwhelm, including those in HCRs. Victims of HCRs are often confused as to why they didn't respond differently or leave. They, too, blame themselves and feel ashamed of what happened. While this is a common human coping technique, it also reflects a misunderstanding of the nervous system's role. Your nervous system is constantly acting for your survival, even when it doesn't make cognitive sense. Understanding this helps us shift our relationship with our nervous system and consider that in these moments of feeling danger or feeling triggered, our nervous system is doing exactly what it was created to do! Letting this sink in can help us step away from self-blame and shame so that at the very least we are not fighting against ourselves.

Internal Safety and Resources

Judith Herman's research found nervous system regulation and internalized safety as the foundational elements of resolving and recovering from trauma.[3] Focusing on the nervous system is the way to establish internalized safety for survivors of trauma. In my own research, I recognized, first, that the nervous system was created to sense danger and threat, which is subjective to each person. And second, I recognized that living in a healing body means learning to recognize when the nervous system is being activated, accepting that it's doing its job, and developing internal resources and safety in the face of activation, threat, and triggers. Noticing our nervous system and developing internal safety is a marker of healing.

While it is true that no one model, approach, or set of approaches works for everyone, we do need a foundation of internal safety (what some might call a felt sense of safety) to move through the trauma resolution and recovery process. If I were to ask if you feel safe inside your body, what would come to mind? For most people who have experienced complex trauma, including religious trauma, the concept and experience of internal safety is new.

When our nervous system is in a constant state of activation, it believes that safety is precluded both internally and externally.

3. Judith Herman, *Trauma and Recovery: The Aftermath of Violence—From Domestic Abuse to Political Terror* (New York: Basic Books, 1992).

Therapist Deb Dana often says that "story follows state."[4] In other words, the state of our nervous system (whether or not we are activated) determines the story we tell ourselves about what is happening in the world around us. If we are stuck on "on," then we tend to see the world as a dangerous and judgmental space that we need to defend ourselves against. If we are stuck on "off," then we tend to experience the world as numb and exhausting. We may isolate ourselves from others to keep from becoming overwhelmed. However, when we can easily move between various nervous system states, including having a sense of internal safety and connection to others, our story shifts to seeing the world and ourselves as inherently good. This means that if our nervous system is constantly activated, then it and our body will rightfully conclude that we are in present danger. In working with trauma, we should first focus on developing a sense of internal calm and safety. Once that is established, then we can offer our body and nervous system other options, including an increased ability to sense that we are no longer in danger. When we no longer feel like we are in danger *and* we have internal resources to shift back into a felt sense of safety, then we have the foundational skills to begin working on resolving our trauma.

To understand both internal safety and internal stability, we need to discuss attachment theory. Attachment theory is a psychological theory recognizing that for normal social and emotional development young children need to have a safe and secure attachment with at least one (primary) caregiver. These connections are a matter of survival because caregivers provide basic needs. Children look to their caregivers not only for food, water, and shelter but also to know that they are loved, connected, accepted, and safe. In practical terms this means that the child can trust the caregiver to be physically present for them and attuned to their

---

4. Deb Dana, "Story Follows State: Climbing the Ladder and Diagnosing," interview with Justin Sunseri, YouTube, August 27, 2019, https://www.youtube.com /watch?v=tUzCnBec-2A.

needs; to help them through mistakes, fear, and uncertainty; and to be the bigger, stronger, wiser, more compassionate adult who can witness, help regulate, and make sense of the little one's moods, emotions, and experiences.

When a child experiences this from their caregiver, they can develop a strong sense of themselves and recognize safe support from others. They can then use what was modeled to them by their caregivers to develop internal resources. The securely attached child's caregiver engages in coregulation—that is, the caregiver helps their child, coaches them, and models to them warm and engaged interactions that fulfill the child's need to "understand, express, and modulate their thoughts, feelings, and behaviors."[5] As a child grows up, they learn to do this for themselves and can often access these skills even when the caregiver is not present. When a child learns that their caregiver can be counted on to protect them, they develop internal safety.

This type of attuned parenting is not required 100 percent of the time. Research indicates that even the best parents are attuned only 30 percent of the time.[6] This is not an invitation or justification for poor behavior, ridicule, or abuse. Rather, this allows parents to be imperfect but still excellent. The other 70 percent of the time parents must be willing to engage in meaningful repair with their child. Meaningful repair includes apologizing, taking ownership/responsibility for how the parent acted, giving age-appropriate consequences, helping the child understand and process what happened, and reestablishing connection. As a caregiver models these behaviors, a child learns how to interact with

---

5. Desiree W. Murray et al., *Self-Regulation and Toxic Stress: Foundations for Understanding Self-Regulation from an Applied Developmental Perspective* (Durham, NC: Center for Child and Family Policy, Duke University, 2015), https://dukespace .lib.duke.edu/dspace/bitstream/handle/10161/10283/report_1_foundations_paper _final_012715.pdf;sequence=1.

6. Lisa Firestone, "Your Child's Self-Esteem Starts with You," *PsychAlive*, accessed January 9, 2023, https://www.psychalive.org/your-childs-self-esteem-starts -with-you/.

others, engage in supportive relationships, not get stuck in a shame cycle, and build safe connections with others.

You may be reading this and feeling dismayed that you didn't experience this type of attuned parenting. Or, in the case of many survivors of HCRs, your caregivers may have been a source of both love and fear as they imparted scary messages and practices and told you that what they were doing or saying came from a place of love. Many clients' parents used corporal punishment for any mistake or sin. Before they were assaulted, many of my clients heard their parents saying something like "I am doing this because I love you" or praying before or after physical punishment. Unfortunately, a child's nervous system is unable to tell the difference between loving assault and dangerous assault. Their nervous system simply registers it as assault—because it is.

When parents are a source of both love and fear, children struggle to form a safe and secure attachment as well as an internalized sense of self, and they grow into adults who live with few internal resources. Additionally, most HCRs teach that people must look to external sources to find safety, direction, and a general sense of being okay. Individuals are not taught to listen to themselves or look inward for any resourcing that may help them feel calm and regulated in times of danger, stress, or other emotional experiences.

When an individual grows up in a family or system that promotes these dynamics, they learn from an early age that life is not safe. They learn that love is conditional, based on compliance and obedience, and that disconnection from God and family will result if they do not live in a specific way. While this might create a "good" child on the outside, the child's internal world is often anything but calm. Without the baseline and modeling from a caregiver to help children work through their experiences, the child must figure out how to be safe in the world on their own. They often do this by adhering to rules, people pleasing, and cutting off parts of themselves that are not in compliance with the system in order to secure their place within the family, the system, or eternity.

Developing Internal Safety after Complex Trauma

In my first session with my somatic therapist, we both assumed that I could access safety within my body. But when she asked me where in my body I felt safe, I stared back at her blankly. Several sessions later she told me that for individuals with CPTSD, the ability to access internal safety had to be created from scratch. Children who did not grow up with caregivers who created safety and stability may fit criteria for complex trauma. Children who grew up with a parent who was a source of both love and fear due to religious teachings and practices often experience dynamics of complex trauma as adults.

When this is the case, building internal safety takes much longer. Our nervous systems thrive on familiarity and stasis. Therefore, even helpful, positive, and safe changes can feel disruptive and must be engaged with in a slow and patient manner. Remember: trauma is the result of anything that is too much, too soon, or too overwhelming. Even something considered "good" can be experienced as negative. Healing from trauma often requires experiencing a response that is the opposite of how you were treated in the traumatic situation. In most cases this means that the slower we go the better, as it gives our bodies time to adapt to these new internal experiences and resolutions.

When looking to develop internal safety with a client who has not experienced this before, therapists often begin by using imagery. For example, I will ask a client to imagine a scene in one of their favorite places on earth (real or imagined) that has no distress, abuse, or trauma associated with it. I encourage them to let themselves be there and to notice what happens in their body. We use this scene as an anchor for what we begin to call "internal safety." We call this internal safety because having a safe landscape shifts our physiology—that is, how we feel and function in our body. When we feel our stress lessen, those feelings are coming from within us. Sometimes this can feel overwhelming because the absence of chaos or nervous system activation might feel so unfamiliar that it's scary. When this is the case, I help my clients take note of it, and I don't ask them to stay in this space longer than a second or two. We then come back to the present moment and talk about the latest episode of their favorite TV show, the weather, or something else benign to help reduce their anxiety, fear response, or other distressing emotions. Even though this feels intolerable, I gently remind them that they gave their body a different experience for one second, which is one second longer than they've had before.

The above activity is one you can try too. As my clients do, notice how your physiology shifts as you imagine this place of calm. If it begins to feel like too much, shift your focus back to the present moment and notice everything in the space around you that is green (or pick a different color). The transition back into the present should help your body feel a bit calmer.

Titration

It is only when the body and nervous system are engaged that healing from religious trauma can begin on the deepest levels. If you are willing to go at the pace of your nervous system, which is usually painstakingly slow at first, your capacity to go faster much sooner will increase. Imagine that you go to the gym for the first time in thirty years. If you begin trying to do bicep curls with one-hundred-pound weights and run ten miles, it's not going to go very well. However, if you start by walking at a relatively easy pace for a half mile on the treadmill and use five-pound weights, not only will it feel more manageable in the moment but you will also feel the impact of the workout in a more tolerable way. Attuning and attending to your nervous system is like this. We don't want to cannonball into a pool that we have never swum in before. Instead, we dip our toe in the water and become familiar with it before we stick another toe in.

Here, the concept of "titration" is helpful. To demonstrate this concept, I like to use an example from high-school chemistry class. When you mix chemicals together, you do it one drop at a time. As you add more of the chemicals together, you observe the reaction to ensure that nothing gets too out of hand. When you know that the reaction is contained, you add another drop and repeat this process. Building a new relationship with your nervous system is similar.

Sometimes even paying attention or being curious about what is happening can feel triggering. The nervous system is constantly scanning for danger, the goal being to keep you alive. Since even positive experiences can feel unfamiliar, your nervous system may perceive them as dangerous. Noticing how long you can do a particular activity before you begin to have intolerable physiological sensations is key. If, for example, in the imagination exercise you notice that after ten seconds you begin to dissociate, feel panic come on, or become enraged, you've found your limit. The next time you try that activity, consider doing it for five to eight seconds before you come back to the present environment and orient yourself to your surroundings. Then, after getting used to the shorter length of time, try adding just one second longer and notice how your body responds. If it is intolerable, pull back again. If not, try adding another second or two the next time.

The Gift of a Stabilized Nervous System

Earlier I stated that I believe fundamentalist religion is a coping mechanism for a dysregulated nervous system. This could be why individuals within HCRs hold so tightly to their beliefs, practices, and lifestyle choices. The lists of dos and don'ts, while often constricting, provide a necessary, albeit temporary, relief in a constantly changing and chaotic world. Though this is merely the illusion of safety, when it's all that is available, we'll take it. On Instagram I asked my followers to share how their lives had changed since befriending and regulating their nervous systems, and I wanted to share some common threads with you:

- I am much more patient with my kids.
- I can handle uncomfortable conversations at work better.
- I no longer feel like I am walking on eggshells with my parents.
- I am much calmer and have healthier communication and relationship with my partner.
- Groups and social experiences are so much easier to participate in.
- It feels safer to feel things as they happen, which lessens the large explosion of repressed pain and emotion.
- I am so much less scared, cautious, and jumpy. I can gently pull my nervous system back from the edge of a "high-activation cliff." I also know how to land softly even if there are activating events; they aren't as terrifying as they used to be.
- Getting my time back! A trigger used to throw me off for hours at best, days at worst. Now I'm able to manage it and get back to things in five to fifteen minutes!
- I now have space for my kids' feelings.

As you can see from these answers, befriending your nervous system, finding a sense of internal safety and stability, and having greater internal capacity to deal with the ups and downs of life is a new way of living. This does not mean that life will be perfect or that you'll never get upset or be triggered again. Shifting your relationship with your nervous system does not take away your humanity! Rather, when we can come from a place of attunement and awareness, we have access to different resources. We will trust ourselves, live from a place of self-compassion, and have a greater sense of self as we interact with the world, which is what the next chapter is all about.

8

Boundaries Built on a Foundation of Self-Trust and Self-Compassion

IN THE THICK OF MY PURITY CULTURE DAYS, I was a boundaries queen. Armed with my list of dos and don'ts, I had a thick hedge of protection around me. I wore my rules like a badge of honor; I liked the feeling of being admired by others when I told them I wasn't going to kiss until I was married.

When I moved to Nashville, I connected with a friend who went to a church every bit as rigid as the one I had come from. However, her theological views contrasted with her warmth and genuine care for others. In casual conversation at a coffee shop, she asked me about my no-kissing rule and gently challenged my notion that it was the most biblical way. I couldn't deny that what she was saying made sense, but it scared me. I recognized that considering her challenge would begin dismantling some deeply held beliefs. I knew that my rules and boundaries would quickly crumble if I agreed that the Bible was unclear about kissing before marriage, and I understood that I would have to start over—without anyone to tell me what was right and wrong in romantic relationships. Despite having no experience with trusting myself, I intuited that taking on her challenge meant that my trust had been misplaced in others and that making others' voices the loudest in my life was not the most effective way to live.

I eventually decided that kissing prior to marriage wasn't a sin; after that, it felt like the bottom of my world fell out from under me. Though my boundaries were primarily focused on romantic relationships, I also used them to evaluate and judge platonic relationships and friendships. In a last-ditch effort to hold on to my rigid boundaries, I reached out to an author who had written a book about being a Christian single woman. While I was delighted that she wrote back, her response was so discouraging, shaming, and filled with resentment toward purity culture that something in me snapped. I had hoped she would encourage me to keep persevering; instead, it was the impetus for leaving the purity culture lifestyle behind. Though I had not yet thoughtfully considered what healthy boundaries would be, I recognized that how I had been living and perceiving the world and relationships up until that point no longer fit who I was becoming.

Boundaries in HCRs

When I was combing through previous research regarding the experience of healing from trauma, the themes of self-trust, self-compassion, and boundaries popped up over and over. In fact, self-trust and self-compassion help create boundaries, and boundaries increase our self-trust and self-compassion. But the boundaries that help people to heal are not those determined by an outside authority. Rather, the boundaries that are core to healing come from a foundation of engagement with the self. These boundaries are rooted in internal clarity and attunement that focuses on an individual's sense of safety in the world with a goal of feeling empowered versus creating lists of what is and is not allowable.

Boundaries, in many HCRs, are composed of lists of rules and behaviors that are prescribed for holy living. While boundaries are loosely discussed for all areas of life, they are primarily used to prescribe rules around sexuality, modesty, sexual activity, emotional intimacy, and gender roles. These rules are derived from spiritual authorities who claim that adherence to these lifestyles equates to holy living.

Within HCRs, boundaries are prescriptive—that is, others outside of yourself create the rules of living. This silences your voice and takes away your ability to choose how you want to live, and it precludes you from developing your own values. In addition, dependence on external authorities can be confusing as the rules can change at any time. Even those who claim to be following the Bible often interpret and apply it quite differently. This can increase fear and feelings of instability as people struggle to understand how to live a godly life. In HCRs, boundaries are composed of binaries. The wrong or bad thing is considered idolatry or giving in to sin. What is considered good or right cannot be questioned and must be adhered to.

Relearning Boundaries

In their research on boundaries, counselors Astra Czerny and Pamela Lassiter found that people benefit from establishing boundaries because they gain a sense of internal empowerment. Czerny and Lassiter define empowerment as a "psychological construct comprised of both internal and external processes that increase awareness of the self, in relationship to others"[1]; they also note

1. Astra B. Czerny and Pamela S. Lassiter, "Healing from Intimate Partner Violence: An Empowerment Wheel to Guide the Recovery Journey," *Journal of Creativity in Mental Health* 11, nos. 3–4 (2016): 314, https://doi.org/10.1080/15401383 .2016.1222321.

that when an individual feels empowered, they can practice boundary flexibility. HCRs require boundary rigidity, or strict and unwavering adherence to all rules with any slight deviation being categorized as sinful. Flexible boundaries, on the other hand, allow an individual to fluidly move along a spectrum between permeability (being open to change or influence) and impermeability based on an individual's internal awareness, attunement to their body, and understanding of their external environment and relationships.[2] Simply put, when boundaries come from a place of empowerment—where an individual can trust themselves and their experience—boundaries can shift and change as an individual shifts and changes over their lifetime.

The process of moving from rigid boundaries to flexible ones is an important part of trauma recovery because it reflects the level of safety a person feels in themselves, their relationships, and the world. As a person's understanding of boundaries moves from an inflexible list of rules defining how to operate in the world to a felt sense of safety and empowerment, trauma survivors gain access to new skills and experiences. As you may have guessed, this theme of healing follows from the previous chapters' themes of embodiment and befriending the nervous system. The more internalized safety and connection a person has with their body, the greater the likelihood that they will feel safe to engage in relationships and in the world in a new way.

It's easy to create an illusion of safety by constructing cut-and-dry rules that prescribe how we must act in the world and how others should act toward us. In other words, when coming out of HCRs, it is common to create expectations for what others should do for us so that we can feel safe in our world. I have empathy

2. Laura E. Anderson, "The Living Experience of Healing the Sexually Traumatized Self" (PhD diss., Saybrook University, 2021), ProQuest (No. 28644488); Astra B. Czerny, Pamela S. Lassiter, and Jae Hoon Lim, "Post-Abuse Boundary Renegotiation: Healing and Reclaiming Self after Intimate Partner Violence," *Journal of Mental Health Counseling* 40, no. 3 (2018): 211–25, https://doi.org/10.17744/mehc.40.3.03.

and compassion for this because I can remember the earnestness with which I sought that for myself. And to be fair, in the early days of healing, a more rigid set of boundaries may be necessary. Above, we discussed how boundaries in HCRs are composed of prescriptive rules, but these boundaries also suggest how a person must show up in the world in order to be loved, accepted, and connected. Clinically speaking, this is the opposite of what boundaries are meant to do. One of the first steps in creating new boundaries is creating a new definition of what boundaries are and what purpose they serve.

After purchasing a new home, one of the first tasks I set out to accomplish was putting in a fence. It offered some much-needed privacy for me, but, more than anything, I wanted my dog to be able to play in the backyard without me having to keep a close eye on her. Within the parameters of the fence, I can see everything going on. Moreover, she is free to roam within the fence. She can play, run around, and bask in the sun, and I can let her do so without worrying that something will happen to her. The fence allows her to have the maximum amount of fun in the safest way possible.

This is how I initially explain boundaries to my clients. Not as a list of things that can and cannot be done but as a yard with a fence around it that provides a sense of safety for the maximum amount of fun and freedom. In this analogy we can decide what does or does not need to be inside the fence for us to feel safe and what needs to stay outside the fence that might feel dangerous. My clients recognize that at the beginning of the healing process they need many items to be inside the parameters of the fence to feel safe, *and* they need many people to remain outside the fence. Often through this practice clients begin to feel safe enough to lean deeper into their process of healing.

Let's do an exercise: Grab a piece of paper and draw a large square. Imagine that the lines of the square are a fence. On the inside of the square write what needs to be present for you to feel safe. For instance, this could mean being able to say no, having the ability to leave somewhere, or having your opinion count. On the outside of the box write down what generally makes you feel unsafe, such as being around people who are quick to judge, feeling unheard, or feeling disrespected. The qualities you write down can help you identify what helps you feel safe or what keeps you from feeling unsafe so that you can establish boundaries. For instance, if "people who are quick to judge" is written outside the fence, then you may need to decrease the time you spend with such people, or you may need to redefine your relationship with folks who demonstrate this quality repeatedly. Alternately, it may be worth exploring relationships or groups of people in which your voice and opinions are valued. Identifying your fences is a great starting point for setting boundaries.

I use this analogy as a starting point because I have found with my clients that as people learn to trust themselves more and rely on themselves for guidance, as a source of insight, and as a meaning maker, it feels safer to expand the fence. Then they can allow others to show up in their own ways without feeling endangered at the first sign of difference, displeasure, or someone else's boundaries and to be open to new experiences and relationships in life.[3] This is where self-trust and self-compassion come in.

HCRs and Self-Judgment

On a warm spring day, I decided to make lunch for myself. I got overly ambitious and decided to take all the ingredients for my lunch from the refrigerator at the same time, and a container of yogurt fell and splattered over the floor. "I'm so stupid, I can't believe I did that! I can't believe how stupid I am," I said to myself.

---

3. Anderson, "Living Experience of Healing."

Whoa. For the first time I heard what I was saying about myself and was appalled. Never, ever would I find it appropriate to speak to someone like this, and yet this was what immediately came to mind when I made a mistake. The words felt familiar though. My mind floated back to my religious days, and I was able to recall several situations in my childhood and as a young adult where that same loud narrative played in my mind as I tried to navigate through my life mistake-free because I believed that mistakes were just one degree away from sin.

The beliefs that we are inherently sinful, that we have no good in us, and that we cannot choose what is good lead us to assume the worst about ourselves and everyone else. An honest mistake is seen as a gross mishandling of a situation. Struggling is evidence of a weak mind, and failing to follow the prescribed ways of living shows our ineptitude in all areas of life. In an HCR, the concept of being kind to oneself is scoffed at because these systems often promote the idea that we don't deserve kindness and that needing anything outside of God can lead us down a slippery slope. One can easily jump from this self-flagellating attitude to being completely devoid of self-trust because self-trust also leads down the same slippery slope.

Here I lean on the amazing work of researchers such as Kristin Neff and Brené Brown, who have devoted their lives to understanding shame, resilience, self-trust, and self-compassion. Both Brown and Neff affirm that developing self-compassion and self-trust shifts how we attune to ourselves and how we move toward others.[4] An additional benefit of developing self-compassion is that it is easier to access compassion for others. Likewise, developing self-trust creates a greater capacity for trusting and engaging with others in a meaningful way.

4. Brené Brown, *Braving the Wilderness: The Quest for True Belonging and the Courage to Stand Alone* (New York: Random House, 2017); Kristin Neff, *Self-Compassion: The Proven Power of Being Kind to Yourself* (New York: William Morrow, 2011).

Self-Compassion

Despite the phenomenal research that Neff has done on self-compassion, we still lack a succinct definition of it. However, Neff describes self-compassion in terms of how we might offer compassion to others. She notes that compassion toward others includes being able to see someone's pain or suffering and being moved by it to respond with warmth and care, to desire to help without judgment, to offer kindness when someone makes a mistake, and to recognize that imperfection is part of the human experience.[5] Self-compassion is the same, except the recipient of this kindness, nonjudgment, and awareness is ourselves. In contrast to the harsh criticism and judgment that HCRs dole out for even minor mistakes and failures, self-compassion champions kindness and understanding when confronted with personal failures, recognizing that no one is perfect.[6] Neff's research recognizes that because self-judgment and self-criticism are so prominent in our culture, we view others with greater skepticism, judgment, and objectification. This in turn causes us to become dishonest and fuels the propensity to hide ourselves because we know that being honest and showing up as ourselves only fuels condemnation.[7] And if this is true of our broader culture, we can imagine the increased severity of it in an HCR, where showing up as ourselves, making a mistake, or sharing an honest thought can carry eternal consequences.

Neff identifies three main components of self-compassion:

- *Self-kindness versus self-judgment*: This includes offering understanding and warmth toward ourselves when we suffer or fail instead of falling into self-criticism. It means

---

5. Kristin Neff, "Self-Compassion: An Alternative Conceptualization of a Healthy Attitude toward Oneself," *Self and Identity* 2 (2003): 85–101, https://self-compassion.org/wp-content/uploads/publications/SCtheoryarticle.pdf.

6. Neff, "Self-Compassion."

7. Neff, "Self-Compassion."

being gentle with ourselves when we are in pain and recognizing that experiencing difficulties is inevitable. When we practice self-kindness, we realize that shaming ourselves or another almost never leads to meaningful change. This perspective contrasts with messages people receive from HCRs.

- *Common humanity versus isolation*: Often when life doesn't go exactly as we want, we may believe we are alone in our suffering. The principle of common humanity recognizes that, as humans, it is common to suffer and that feeling inadequate is part of the human experience. Unlike in HCRs, which teach that suffering is a result of sin, human unworthiness, and human flaws, self-compassion promotes a realization that we are not alone in our suffering.

- *Mindfulness versus over-identification*: This component focuses on the balance of acknowledging what is happening and what we are feeling without suppressing or exaggerating what is going on. This includes being able to observe ourselves without judgment and without denying or getting stuck in what is happening. In HCRs people commonly overidentify with the idea of being a sinner in need of a savior. This perception then colors how we see ourselves and others and how we navigate the world; it also shifts our purpose.[8]

Though the goal of Neff's work on self-compassion is not specifically geared toward boundary making, the components of self-compassion that she describes do allow for boundaries to be built that will create a greater sense of safety and that will allow people to show up authentically in the world. For instance, HCRs promote

8. Kristin Neff, "What Self-Compassion Is," Self-Compassion.org, accessed January 10, 2022, https://self-compassion.org/the-three-elements-of-self-com passion-2/#3elements.

being suspicious and untrusting of people based on the notion that they are inherently sinful. Therefore, a person's words and actions are met with skepticism and doubt, as those around them are assuming the worst about them. Practicing self-compassion allows us to recognize the humanity in ourselves and others and to practice kindness. We may still require boundaries, but we can do so without assuming that others are set on harming or exploiting us. As we heal, our boundaries can become more open and can reflect a restored view of the goodness of both ourselves and others.

Self-Trust

"Trust" is often an ambiguous word. What does it mean when we say we don't trust someone? This is the question that Brené Brown sets out to answer. In her work, she uses Charles Feltman's definitions of "trust" and "distrust." He defines trust as "choosing to risk making something you value vulnerable to another person's actions" and distrust as "what's important to me is not safe with this person in this situation (or any situation)."[9] Brown acknowledges that even with this definition, trust can mean many things to many people so her aim is to explore the components of trust. Her research identifies seven key components of trust (elements that are present in a trusting relationship), and she acknowledges that while these components of trust invite connection with others, they are also a tool to invite connection with oneself. When difficulties occur, our initial thought toward ourselves is often one covered in shame and distrust ("I can't believe I did that!" "I can't trust myself!").[10] Brown identifies and defines the following components of trust and explains how they relate to self-trust.

9. Charles Feltman, *The Thin Book of Trust: An Essential Primer for Building Trust at Work* (Bend, OR: Thin Book Publishing, 2009), 7.
10. Brown, *Braving the Wilderness*, 37–39.

- *Boundaries*: I respect my boundaries, and when I'm not clear about what's okay and not okay, I reflect. I'm willing to say, "No." Do I respect my own boundaries? Was I clear about what's okay and not okay?

- *Reliability*: You do what you say you'll do. This means staying aware of your competencies and limitations so you don't overpromise and are able to deliver on commitments and balance competing priorities. Am I reliable? Do I do what I said I was going to do?

- *Accountability*: You own your mistakes, apologize, and make amends. Do I own *my* mistakes, apologize, and make amends?

- *Vault*: You don't share information or experiences that are not yours to share. Do I respect the vault for myself and for others? Do I share appropriately?

- *Integrity*: You choose courage over comfort. You choose what is right over what is fun, fast, or easy. And you choose to practice your values rather than simply professing them. Do I act from a place of integrity?

- *Nonjudgment*: I can ask for what I need, and others can ask for what they need. We can talk about how we feel without judgment. Do I ask for what I need? Am I nonjudgmental toward myself about needing help? You cannot judge yourself for needing help and not judge others for needing help!

- *Giving the most generous assumption*: You extend the most generous interpretation possible to the intentions, words, and actions of yourself—giving the benefit of the doubt. Do I give myself the benefit of the doubt? Am I generous in my assumptions about myself?[11]

11. Brené Brown, "SuperSoul Sessions: The Anatomy of Trust," video series, November 1, 2015, https://brenebrown.com/videos/anatomy-trust-video/.

When I work with clients to develop self-trust and boundaries, I often have them review this list and identify *one* area that they want to begin working on since they usually say that all of them need work. As we develop these components within the frame of self-trust, they extend outward, affecting both boundaries and other relational dynamics. People learn to better identify why they struggle with certain people, why others appeal to them, and how to ask for what they need in a relationship. Unlike Neff's work, Brown's work does see boundaries as one of the outcomes of self-trust. In fact, Brown suggests that boundaries are part of trusting oneself. Likewise, the more someone can trust in and rely on themselves, the more they can create boundaries that reflect their highest value and allow others to do the same.

Boundaries, Self-Compassion, and Self-Trust

Self-compassion and self-trust are important for another piece of healing as well: allowing ourselves space and permission to consider that each of us are doing the best that we can with the resources we have available to us. I have had the privilege of speaking with many former and/or deconstructed clergy members who have expressed an enormous amount of sadness and regret for the way they taught and treated people while they were in an HCR. Part of their healing includes processing grief for how they participated in and perpetuated the system of abuse. Many of us, even those who were not in formal leadership positions, feel this same regret. Because of this, developing self-compassion and self-trust become even more important. When we can offer ourselves compassion for how we handled things and participated in harmful practices inside these systems of power and control, the consequences may not go away, but we may be able to release any intense shame we may feel. When we seek to develop self-trust, we give ourselves the opportunity to operate from a different set of values and with integrity.

Within my research, I give a raw description of the process of moving from a place of shame, self-hatred, and outsourcing of trust to self-compassion and self-trust:

> There wasn't something wrong with me; I wasn't trying to be destructive. There was just no way I could have possibly known how to do anything different. I had literally no self-worth or value because they had taken it away and told me that my worth and value came from outside myself. I couldn't trust myself or my intuition because they told me how evil I was, inherently, and I would never choose good if left to my own. I had no opinion or voice because they told me that mine didn't matter. I had no idea my body even existed because they told me it was evil and I needed to kill it. I didn't know how to make choices because they told me everything was prescribed. It is not my fault that I did not know how to function in the world after thirty-plus years of psychological, emotional, verbal, sexual, and spiritual abuse.[12]

My research revealed that as the healing process continues a relationship of burgeoning self-trust allows for tenderness and compassion that were not previously accessible. When I explore this theme with clients, they often report that people around them notice this change almost immediately. They begin to be perceived differently. Others experience them as more confident, they feel they can display empathy without getting over-involved, and they feel able to offer a sense of tenderness to themselves and others that is both different and inspirational.

Finally, as mentioned briefly above and as affirmed by other research, boundaries that stem from a place of self-compassion and self-trust must involve connecting to our body. HCRs disconnect us from our body and therefore disconnect us from very important information regarding what feels good and safe. Becoming embodied and tuning in to our nervous system allows us to

12. Anderson, "Living Experience of Healing."

become aware of both how our body is experiencing a situation as well as what our body might need for safety—essentially, where the boundary needs to be created. It's important to listen to cues from our body. For example, a feeling of resistance or openness, an elevated heart rate or a feeling of peace, or a quickening or deepening of breath can give us cues as to how safe our body feels and where the boundaries may need to be established or renegotiated.

Putting It Together in Real Life

When I decided that kissing before marriage was not a sin, I struggled to know what my new boundaries would be. Without someone directing my steps and without the fear of punishment for engaging in various premarital sexual activities, I felt lost. Boundaries, to me, were still the lists of dos and don'ts rather than a reflection of my values that came from within. Over a period of several years, I often would give myself a rule to follow and then feel extreme guilt for not following that rule. While I never felt guilty about what I did, I felt guilty that I didn't do what I said I was going to do. It wasn't until I began to cultivate self-compassion and develop a sense of inner trust that I was able to transform the choices I made. Still, something was missing. I had become dismayed at how my best intentions seemed to bring about more hurt and confusion. While I no longer desired the "boundaries" I had while in the HCR I was part of, I did long for the confidence and certainty I had when I communicated and stuck to my boundaries, despite what others thought. That felt almost . . . easy. Despite trusting myself, having compassion toward myself, and living in a way that reflected my value and worth, I still feared disappointing someone or making them feel uncomfortable.

Then, during the last couple hours of an intensive trauma training, a friend of mine and I requested to be in the same practice session. The activity seemed simple enough: we would stand a distance apart from each other and the person in the role of the therapist would ask if they could take a step closer to the person who was in the role of the client. The client would check in with their body and deliver an answer according to what they were internally sensing. In a joking way, my friend and I told our assistant that we would probably be in each other's faces given how safe we felt with each other. But when my turn came to be in the role of the client and my friend asked if he could take a step forward, my body indicated a strong *no*. He asked if I would like to take a step back, and I felt a strong *yes*, so I moved backward. In the entirety of the exercise, he only got a half step closer to me, but as he respected my *no* and offered compassion, empathy, and understanding instead of questions, coercion, and impatience, my bodily sensations began to shift. A long-dormant strength reemerged, and confidence settled back into my body. I felt completely different.

I've repeated that exercise with clients, and each time they are astounded by the wisdom of their bodies and the radical shifts that happen when they are encouraged to trust themselves and speak from that place. When I ask some of my clients and others what it's like to have boundaries based on a sense of self-trust and compassion, they share the following:

- "It doesn't feel as terrifying to ask for what I want or to tell someone what I don't want."
- "I know the difference between not wanting to do something because it feels unsafe or just because it's uncomfortable. Then can decide if I want to stretch myself."
- "I feel like my actions are congruent with my values, and I am so much kinder to myself even when I make a mistake!"
- "Talking to my parents doesn't feel as scary anymore— I've told them which topics are off-limits and redirected the conversation if we get close to those topics. I've found that there are many other things we can easily talk about that create a pleasant relationship."

- "My partner and my children feel safer to me—I don't believe they are trying to make my life harder, and my kids have been able to learn how to set their own boundaries and ask for what they want."

- "I've actually lost a lot of friendships because I realized that they were friends with me because of what they could get from me. But the friends that stuck around are the ones I want to have in my life forever."

- "My partner and I have been able to become more adventurous sexually because we trust each other's intentions and communicate if things feel too overwhelming or unsafe. When that happens, we pause and reconnect to help each other and ourselves feel safe again."

- "My body lets me know when social media becomes too activating by physiological cues, and when I listen to my body, I feel a deeper sense of trust in myself."

Here is one final thing to consider as we close this chapter: unlike boundaries in HCRs that are rigid and fixed (meaning unchanging), living in a healing body means that boundaries can and should change over time as you grow and change. What you need to feel safe today may be different from what you needed a year ago, and in a year from now it might be different still. Moreover, our boundaries can change depending on the person(s) we are with, our stage of life, our level of stress, or any other factor. They can even change from one day to the next! The beauty of being able to use our inner landscape to notice what feels good and safe means that the kinder we are to ourselves and the more trust we develop, the more we can recognize what we need in each moment to live from a place of understanding our value.

9

Grieving the Life
You Once Had

ON A CRISP, sunny Sunday afternoon, I set out on my hiking trail
ready to process some issues. The greenway is my place for self-
therapy and the place I feel safest in my body and the world. I had
been working through some issues involving my former boss and
pastor, Tray, the role he played in my life, and the effect he had.
The end of my time working for him had always confused me. I
couldn't wrap my head around why he had been so angry about my
wanting to date a fellow youth leader. As I walked on the trail, I felt
anger rising in my body and knew that the anger was a messenger
telling me that something wasn't right—that what happened to
me wasn't okay. Truthfully, until that point, I hadn't focused on
the details of what happened or how it affected me, but memories
had been resurfacing recently, which I took as an indication that
my body was ready to resolve what was still living inside me.

I replayed scenes and conversations from years before but this
time it felt like I was watching on a movie screen. Suddenly I realized that Tray had not actually been mad at me for who I was dating;
instead, he was mad because I said no to his control over my life. I

went against his counsel as my spiritual authority, prioritized another man over him, decided to think for myself, and made my own choices. And then I paid, with my job, my community, my friends, my mentors, my credibility, and my reputation all being taken away.

For years I blamed myself for everything that happened. I wrote Tray multiple letters taking ownership for every part. I analyzed everything that happened to ensure that I accurately understood what I had done and how much I had sinned—blaming and shaming myself, even after ceasing all contact with him.

On the trail though, I saw each action I took and attempt I made at repentance and reconciliation on the movie screen that was playing in my mind, but I saw it now through a fresh set of eyes. And then it was as if the movie kept playing and I was able to see the effect this relationship had on me well over a decade later. I could see how his treatment of me was psychologically and spiritually abusive. I saw how his authority in my life had divorced me from myself. By this point I was at a spot on the hiking trail that not many others frequented, so I imagined Tray was there with me, and I let him have it. Anger that I didn't even know was there bubbled up and out. I yelled at him until my voice grew hoarse. And then deep sadness came. I began to weep for the burden I had carried that was not mine, for the ways I shamed and blamed myself, for the ways I took ownership and responsibility, and for the ways I had to fragment myself to survive. I grieved for how I had believed that this spiritual authority was unequivocally right and how this experience had changed me on every level, including changing the course of my life.

Cultural and Religious Notions of Grief

Culturally and religiously speaking, grief is often associated with loss. Historically, in therapeutic spaces, grief is recognized as a necessary process for bereavement, which includes various stages one moves through on the way to acceptance. In religious contexts, grief is not often considered appropriate. In most cases, the only time we're allowed to express grief is following the death of a loved one. The most recent version of the American Psychological Association's diagnostic manual (*DSM-5-TR*) includes a new diagnosis called "prolonged grief disorder" (also called "complicated grief")—that is, grief that lasts for an extended period and affects various aspects of a person's life.

Though it is rarely explicitly stated within an HCR, such communities often have expectations for how a person grieves, including why and how long one can grieve and what spiritual judgments are made if a person grieves longer than the appropriate time. In an HCR, people are often told that their loved one is in heaven or that they are no longer suffering on earth or that they will see them again one day. This is called spiritual bypassing.

Spiritual bypassing is a tool used to sidestep complicated emotions, psychological issues, and unfinished developmental tasks. (Of course, spiritual bypassing happens outside HCRs and is used in contexts other than death.) Religions use this tool to circumvent the grieving process and to avoid difficult emotions. As we will discuss in the next chapter, in HCRs emotions are considered unnecessary at best and sinful at worst. Many HCRs instill in their followers a fear that if they grieve for too long, even after a loved one has died, their emotions will take over. Instead, HCRs offer platitudes to get people to look on the bright side so that others around them can avoid feeling their own discomfort with grief and loss. Focus is instead placed on seeing what people can learn through the experience or what God might be teaching them. Rather than dealing with difficult emotions or painful experiences, many are taught to instead look for how God can use the situation to bring glory to his name.

Traumatic Grief

Neslihan Arici Özcan and Mehmet Kaya coined the term "traumatic grief." This is grief in which an individual "had to learn to adapt to a new life due to the traumatic circumstances impacting their relationships, career, physical and mental health, and even economic experiences."[1] The term "traumatic grief" recognizes that not all trauma results in death and instead focuses on various aspects of loss. It recognizes that grief often stems from loss due to what has happened, even if the loss is not related to the death of a specific person.[2] Traumatic grief impacts an individual in every dimension; an important piece of trauma recovery is allowing the body to move through the grieving process in a trauma-informed way. Grief produces stress in the body that may compound the traumatic stress that is already present. The concept of traumatic grief is useful in the discussion of living in a healing body after religious trauma.

I met with a client who had grown up in an HCR that required her to cut off parts of herself to survive the physical, emotional, spiritual, and verbal abuse that was doled out by her pastor, who was also her father. She relayed the shock and horror she felt when she realized how many life-altering decisions she made based on a version of God that she no longer believed in. Though she deeply loved her numerous children, she quietly admitted that she never actually wanted to be a mother. Instead, she had dreams of traveling, doing advocacy work, and focusing on a career in helping others. Now, in her late forties with several mouths to feed, a mortgage, a shaky marriage, and a body that was giving out on her due to her demanding job, she was angry at how much of her life was the result of choices that others made for her.

I have heard this story, in some fashion, hundreds of times. People express bitter acceptance as they recognize the life they

1. Neslihan Arici Özcan and Mehmet Kaya, "The Effectiveness of Family Resiliency Program with Traumatic Grief on Women's Post-Traumatic Stress, Grief and Family Resiliency Level," *Education and Science* 44, no. 197 (2019): 121, https://www.proquest.com/docview/2186801113.
2. Laura E. Anderson, "The Living Experience of Healing the Sexually Traumatized Self" (PhD diss., Saybrook University, 2021), ProQuest (No. 28644488).

have lost, the choices they were unable to make, and the parts of themselves they had to cut off to survive—all of which landed them in the present moment and contributed to their feelings of being confined and unable to escape their life. As I helped another client sift through the available choices, given all he had gone through, he quietly wondered, "Does choice even exist when I'm having to make decisions based on choices that others made for me years ago?" I wish I could say I had the perfect response for him in that moment, but the only answer was for me to sit with him in this heavy realization.

As I've worked with clients and consulted with other trauma practitioners, I've learned that grieving the life we once had often falls into five categories: our childhood/adolescence, our education, our sexuality, our view of others and the world, and grieving the good.

Grieving Our Childhood and Adolescence

Though each HCR offers certain nuances regarding what is expected from and taught to children and teenagers, an overwhelming theme of arrested development is present. Depending on the context, children's development is either stunted or accelerated, often both, to fit the teachings of the religion. In some cases, this might include infantilizing children—that is, acting and treating them as if they are incapable of doing anything for themselves. In other cases, children are parentified, which means that at young ages they are required to take on parental and adult responsibilities, such as helping to raise their siblings and serving their parents. Children within these systems are typically taught that they cannot trust themselves. This creates a dependency on their parents and often keeps them from developing a sense of autonomy and individuality.

There are normal and appropriate developmental milestones for sexuality, various forms of intelligence, and social engagement.

However, within HCRs these areas are often stunted, dismissed, or vilified. This might look like punishing a child for natural sexual exploration, preventing children from going to school, or sheltering a child from the outside world, all of which stunt a child's ability to learn social cues and develop relationships.

Grieving a stunted or accelerated childhood and adolescence is a complex process. People often feel shock and shame as they slowly peel back the layers of what they missed out on or how they have been miseducated. If you experienced this, you may feel like you have a lot of work to do to get "up to speed" on various educational subjects, pop-culture references, and the nuances of human interaction. You may feel overwhelmed, angry, or sad. For this kind of grieving, I discuss the idea of an "inner child" with my clients, and we engage in activities, conversations, and practices of curiosity that were not afforded them when they were younger.

Inner-child work is a pop-psychology term that is most closely associated with the therapeutic model known as internal family systems. In this work we recognize that parts of us are stuck in past ways of reacting, feeling, thinking, and believing. This does not mean we have multiple personalities; instead, it refers to common language we hear or use in everyday conversation. For example, we've all said something like, "Part of me feels x, and another part of me feels y." Inner-child work suggests that the parts of us that are stuck in the past are younger versions of ourselves—our child selves. In inner-child work the goal is to help our inner child feel safe and to reparent them with our adult, present-day self acting as the kind and loving parent. This is often accomplished through internal dialogue, play, laughter, expressing emotion, and interacting with that child self in the same way we would with an actual child. Sometimes this means focusing on basic needs; other times it may require unburdening the inner child from coping mechanisms we had to use as a child but that are no longer helpful.

Grieving Our Education

Tara Westover's highly acclaimed book, *Educated*, details her experience of growing up with survivalist parents in the mountains of Idaho. Due to her parents' beliefs, she lived in extreme isolation and was prevented from receiving an education. When she was seventeen, Tara entered a formal classroom and was introduced to a world of knowledge and possibilities for the first time. While her experience is viewed as fringe or extreme, it is common in HCRs. In some cases, depending on various factors like gender, body ability, or skin color, people may be denied education past a certain point or altogether.

One client relayed to me that they had to start assuming that literally everything they had been told was wrong and that the opposite was true. Like in grieving a childhood and adolescence, many of my clients feel shame and embarrassment in this area because they don't know basic information that many other people learned in school. Many of my clients grieve what was lost as they recognize how this directly impacted their choices for careers, future goals, and even relationships.

Grieving Our Sexuality

When I teach about sexual development, I use an example of a dimmer switch. We are born as sexual beings, which means that this part of us develops over time. As we get older, our sexuality "light" gets brighter in age-appropriate ways. Age-appropriate sexual development is a natural progression that should feel good and safe. However, in some cases—among them those where sexual abuse occurs or where sexual development is stunted, such as in many HCRs—sexuality is viewed as a regular on-and-off light switch. The switch is to be kept off until we enter a legal, lifelong, heterosexual marriage. However, since normal sexual development has been bypassed or stifled, our bodies often interpret sexual arousal as dangerous. Therefore, when individuals eventually engage in sexual activity, many of them who were given an on-off view of sexuality have physiological responses similar to those who have survived sexual assault. These can include physical pain during sex, guilt, shame, and anxiety around engaging in sex, feelings of disgust toward sex or engaging in sex, inability to orgasm, and dissociating during sexual experiences.

Additionally, many people who grew up in an HCR were taught that anything outside of male or female identities and heterosexual relationships is a sin. Individuals whose identities do not fit these narrow categories are required to suppress their sexuality and often the essence of who they are to avoid sin and to be accepted in the group. While most fundamentalist religions require suppression of everyone's sexuality, those who don't fit inside the prescribed gender and sexuality box experience a unique set of long-lasting effects, such as internalized homophobia, immense shame, self-hatred, isolation, and sometimes self-harm and suicide.

After leaving an HCR, it's not uncommon for someone to swing to the opposite side of the spectrum regarding sexual behavior. Due to the lack of progressive sexual development and sexual education outside of encouragement to be abstinent, many people engage in risky behaviors, do not understand consent, are assaulted or violated, or do not know how to practice safer sex. This dynamic often adds to the process of grieving as they may feel reckless, scared, or out of control, and they have a greater chance of experiencing long-lasting effects because of their arrested sexual development and education.

Grieving Our View of Others and the World

HCRs are, by nature, exclusive. While that may sound bizarre given their proselytizing nature, there are very clear rules and practices to establish who is in and who is out. In some ways, being on the outside of this system makes someone dangerous simply because they are on the outside of the system and do not pay attention to the specific beliefs and complexities of an HCR member they may interact with. In other cases, the hierarchy inside the system is projected to the external world and people's value is determined by external factors such as gender or race. Sometimes an HCR does not grant the same access, privileges, or resources to all group members. This can be confusing for members who are equally as committed to the group as others who have greater privileges. People often don't realize that HCRs create a hierarchy within the group that determines how safe or dangerous a person is, how much they should be listened to, whether they should be believed, and how seriously their (negative) actions should be taken.

This dynamic and the grief that often results goes back to our discussion of how AREs are related to patriarchy and systems of oppression. Many of my clients have expressed deep remorse, sadness, and anger as they have come to recognize how they were conditioned to view people who are different from themselves. The process of grieving involves untangling these systems in our own bodies (see chap. 5 under the heading "Embodied Fundamentalism") so that we can not only ensure that we don't switch from one fundamentalist belief system to another, but also so that we can have a more compassionate view of others.

Grieving the Good

Traumatic grief isn't simply grieving what we missed out on; it also includes grieving the loss of positive experiences and connections we once had. Unequivocally when I ask people what they miss the most about their former life, they say community. Having a group of people to turn to who share our beliefs, values, and life is often one of the most appealing parts of a religious system—and the one people miss the most when they leave. In her book *The Struggle to Stay*, Katie Gaddini explores the experience of single evangelical women and their reasons for staying with or leaving their churches. When she asked research participants what keeps them from leaving, every participant listed community as a driving factor. Gaddini herself grew up in evangelicalism before leaving religion entirely as an adult. She acknowledges the beautiful sense of community she felt within evangelicalism: "You'll never find a suitable replacement, no matter how hard you look."[3] The hole that Gaddini and many others feel after leaving an HCR is gaping, and the grief is real.

It is easy for humans to understand binaries. When we think about HCRs, we would prefer to think of them as all good or all bad. The problem with this mentality, however, is that if something was all bad, all the time, then it's unlikely we would have become involved or stayed. I believe it's important to recognize the good aspects—as well as what we might miss when we leave. Grieving involves allowing ourselves to be honest, and most of us had some good, even transformational, moments in the HCR we were part of. I led worship for many years, and that's something I truly miss. I love singing and playing the piano, and my departure from religion meant that regular and communal singing was no longer a part of my norm. I grieve this loss.

It's perfectly acceptable to miss some of the conveniences of HCRs as well. Many of these systems provided meals, activities for children, babysitting services, retreats, and learning opportunities that were lifesavers. Religious systems also offer access to generational diversity that allows individuals to engage in relationships that can be incredibly fulfilling and that are unmatched in organizations outside the system. For single mothers, especially, the religious system provides essential needs, such as physical, financial, and relational support that make the system both appealing and relieving—and this loss can feel insurmountable.

---

3. Katie Gaddini, *The Struggle to Stay: Why Single Evangelical Women Are Leaving the Church* (New York: Columbia University Press, 2022), 174.

Finally, religious systems offer a sense of certainty. Many times, I post a question on social media and invite people to ask me questions about religious trauma and healing. One of the questions I receive quite often is about how to deal with the lack of certainty after you deconstruct your religion or leave it altogether. Without the certainty of religion, many people experience significant anxiety as they try to find a sense of groundedness. Even if religion or religious beliefs no longer make sense to you cognitively, it's still okay to miss and even wish for the certainty you previously had in that religion.

Denial

Though I do not subscribe to specific stages of grief or a specific process for grief, I find it important to consider how denial and grief go together and how being honest about denial is essential to living as a healing individual. This is the definition of denial that I use: denial is a defense mechanism that keeps us from seeing things how they truly are/were, because if we did see them for how they truly are/were, it would feel consciously intolerable.

For another way to think about this, we can use blinders as an analogy. At some point in our life we live with blinders on. Imagine the blinders that horses wear when they are pulling a carriage in the park. These blinders limit their vision, allowing them to see only what is in front of them. Our blinders can be like that too. Whether out of ignorance or willfulness, we often live in our own version of the world. This is a common coping mechanism because we intuitively know that if we didn't have those blinders, we may be shocked at what we see. In HCRs, blinders keep people alive because they allow people to maintain adherence to the rules and beliefs, in many cases without question, and remain connected to the group.

Grieving the life that we lost begins with removing the blinders and being willing to look at what we have not previously allowed ourselves to see. This often means we begin seeing various aspects of life differently than in the past. It may include seeing how certain beliefs are harmful, hypocritical, or dehumanizing. It may include seeing how we have had to fragment ourselves, ignore our bodies, and silence ourselves. It may include seeing systems of oppression and patriarchy and the effects they have on individuals and entire groups of people. It may include seeing the various distortions and lies you have had to believe to survive this type of environment and reckoning with how they still live inside you.

When we allow ourselves to face denial—that is, to see things as they truly are/were—it's normal to feel angry. Our anger tells us that what happened to us was not okay. We don't get angry about things that don't matter. When we begin to see life outside the bill of goods that was previously sold to us, it's natural to feel angry, duped, and betrayed. While I don't advocate destructive behavior toward self or others because of anger, it's important to notice the anger you feel because it shows you what is most important to you and what you are most passionate about (see chap. 10 for more on emotions).

Acceptance

To end this chapter, I want to talk about acceptance. According to Elisabeth Kübler-Ross's five stages of grief, acceptance is the last stage in the grieving process. In my experience, many people look at this stage and believe that reaching it means they are healed and will never feel sad again about what has been lost. Yet Kübler-Ross's grief model was not intended for survivors of the one who has died. Her stages of grief were developed for people with long-term illnesses who understood that death was coming quicker than they might like. Acceptance was the fifth and final stage of her model and was intended to help people live in a meaningful way as they were dying. Her model may also help those who are grieving certain losses in their life due to involvement in an HCR.

The model was intended to help those grieving to create meaning for the life they have before them.[4]

Acceptance is not an end point like a period at the end of a sentence. Rather, acceptance allows us to acknowledge what happened and, in most cases, to acknowledge that it wasn't okay. Acceptance means allowing yourself to be present in each moment, allowing yourself to feel how you feel, and to move on to the next moment. Acceptance doesn't mean you have to forgive, repair relationships, or pretend that you are fine. Acceptance means leaning into the present moment and letting the truth that comes from that heal you. Acceptance happens when we allow the blinders to come off and see things with accuracy and honesty.

When we offer ourselves this alternate meaning of acceptance, we may find that what seemed to have the most power over us seems a little bit less powerful. This often allows us to move even closer to being the person we want to become, rather than being so deeply defined by what happened to us. Acceptance doesn't mean that we forget what happened, and it doesn't mean that the pain of what happened is gone, never to return. It simply means that the pain, hurt, abuse, and trauma do not become our identity, and we are able to move forward in freedom.

4. Elisabeth Kübler-Ross, *On Death and Dying* (New York: Macmillan, 1970).

10

Developing a Robust
Spectrum of Emotions

AS A YOUNG CHILD I was regularly punished for emotional outbursts. Any emotional expression that was deemed too much was not believed to be authentic and was dismissed. Even when a sibling would hurt me, I would be told to minimize my pain and calm down; I was told it wasn't that bad. I eventually learned that my "heart"—a code word used to refer to emotions—was deceitful. As I grew older these messages were echoed by others in my life who told me I was too much, too emotional, and a lot to handle. The heavy weight of these statements was too great to bear, so I learned how to dampen my emotions and developed religious scrupulosity as a way to manage my feelings.

I was introduced to the Enneagram after moving to Nashville. I sat in a coffee shop with a therapist-friend who agreed to teach me more about it. When he asked me what number resonated the most, I indicated a type 1: the perfectionist. Puzzled, he gently shared that he didn't experience me as a type 1. As I learned more about the Enneagram, I found myself loathing type 4s. They were emotional, passionate, swept up into fantasy and imagination—a far cry from being measured, practical, efficient, and from having an inner critic that wouldn't shut up. I thought I must be a type 1. I was the person who could handle extra work and short deadlines and who would pick up the slack when others couldn't do their part. I was harsh and critical toward myself, and I felt let down when others couldn't keep up with me. But I also felt like I was wearing a mask. As I continued my own healing work, I felt less like a type 1. At one point I commented to my therapist that I was either the healthiest type 1 in the entire world, or I wasn't a type 1. And while I was proud of the work I had done on myself, the latter option seemed more plausible.

One day as I listened to an Enneagram podcast, I heard a type 4 description that felt like a case study of my life. I was shocked. A type 4? Those moody, emotional, self-absorbed, sadness-loving people? And yet I couldn't deny that when I was honest with myself, this was who I was. As I reflected on my life, I saw my internal world with fresh eyes. I noticed how many parts of myself I'd had to cut off to survive. I had to fragment passion, creativity, empathy, depth—even acknowledging that I felt comfortable in the dark spaces! By acknowledging these dormant parts of myself, I began to develop emotions and expressions that were previously hidden. I became fluent in feeling again.

Cutting Off Our Emotions

In their studies on the impact of trauma, Bessel van der Kolk, Peter Levine, and Judith Herman all affirm that the extreme overwhelm that leads to trauma often includes being cut off from one's emotions.[1] Drawing from their work in my dissertation, I wrote that "inability to access emotions may be due to dissociation/freeze,

1. Judith Herman, *Trauma and Recovery: The Aftermath of Violence—From Domestic Abuse to Political Terror* (New York: Basic Books, 1992); Peter Levine, *Waking the Tiger: Healing Trauma* (Berkeley: North Atlantic Books, 1997); Bessel van der

feelings of numbness, or fearing the vulnerability that emotions may cause."[2] In the context of an HCR, where one is often required to be in a constant state of activation, cutting off emotions is billed as holy and godly. Any emotional expression, then, may feel scary because of how unfamiliar it feels in a person's body and may cause them to doubt their faith and eternal security.

In therapeutic communities, thoughts are considered to be the language of the mind and emotions are the language of the body. Emotions are experienced in the body, and when they're ignored, they can become overwhelming to feel or express. In chapter 6, I noted that many HCRs require individuals to divorce themselves from their bodies and to move exclusively into their minds. That information is also applicable here, as one can naturally conclude that if the body is vilified, then the language that the body speaks must also be vilified. Jeremiah 17:9 says that the heart is deceitful above all things. While many HCRs emphasize the mind and will over the body and emotions, some religious denominations accept emotional experiences. However, this doesn't always extend to the full spectrum of emotions; instead, emotions that are deemed acceptable are usually positive in nature and are directed toward God or involve how one feels about God. Admitting anger, sadness, or frustration toward God is usually not welcomed and is often considered alarming.

Though I cannot be certain of all the reasons why emotions seem dangerous, I am struck that, in many cases, the emotion-body connection tells a different story than what is being taught in an HCR. I think back to my first sexual experience where I expected to feel immense guilt and shame. And yet my body told a different story—so much so that I could not deny the sharp contrast between my lived experience and the messages I had been taught.

Kolk, *The Body Keeps the Score: Brain, Mind, and Body in the Healing of Trauma* (New York: Penguin Books, 2015).

2. Laura E. Anderson, "The Living Experience of Healing the Sexually Traumatized Self" (PhD diss., Saybrook University, 2021), ProQuest (No. 28644488), 140.

Deciding to listen to the different story that the body and emotions tell, rather than listening to doctrine or rules, decreases the influence of a spiritual authority. This is one reason HCRs may find the body and emotions to be so dangerous and instead use shame as a way to gain power and control.

Developing Shame

In chapter 7, I introduced attachment theory and discussed how safe attachment as modeled by an attuned caregiver allows a child to learn how to feel safe in the world. How to deal with and feel emotions is part of what a caregiver models. As children, we are helpless in almost all ways. This means that we need an adult who is bigger, stronger, wiser, more nurturing, and more compassionate, who can allow us to be kids while maintaining a structure that prioritizes safety and helps us learn to regulate emotions. For example, if a child is throwing a temper tantrum, they need an adult who can help them calm down rather than an adult who has a tantrum with them. Some clinicians have used attachment theory to develop what's called the circle of security. This therapeutic intervention is designed to help parents understand their role in their child's life as it pertains to developing a secure attachment. When kids feel securely attached, they know they will be protected, comforted, delighted in, and will have a place to organize their feelings and experiences.

When children do not receive this type of parenting, it is often due to a parent not receiving this type of parenting from their parents. How someone's parents demonstrated attachment to them along with parenting messages they received within an HCR often create parents who are ill-equipped to offer safe attachment and emotional regulation to their own children. This helps us understand why our parents did what they did while still validating our experiences. When a parent cannot offer their child safety and emotional regulation, the child is left to make meaning of their parent's actions and to shift in an attempt to get their basic need for secure attachment met. A child is unable to understand that their parents may never have been taught parenting skills, may be living out of their own pain or shame, or would suffer grave consequences for not raising their child within specific standards. The child, instead, can make sense of this only by assuming that *they* are the problem. This forces children to shut down their emotions, to internalize pain, and to live from shame.

Unfortunately, even after a child turns eighteen and leaves the family home or deconstructs their experience in an HCR, the coping mechanisms they used to navigate overwhelming situations as a child do not go away. For these children-turned-adults, shame is often the most effective coping mechanism because shutting down emotions, internalizing pain, and assuming that something is wrong with them has become the most effective way to live. This dynamic often leads to reactive adults in the present day. Even if we can cognitively understand why we were disconnected from our emotions, we may not be able to translate that into healthy emotional expression. The impact of this is vast and includes how we attach to others, engagement in codependent behaviors, projection, introjection, and how we view ourselves. One of the most noticeable ways this can affect an individual is through emotional development.

Emotional Development

Developing a robust spectrum of emotions happens over time. We do not get to pick and choose which emotions to feel and which emotions to numb and discard. Numbing or discarding some emotions means numbing or discarding all emotions.[3] Cutting off pain also cuts off our access to joy. In HCRs this cutting off is done to

---

3. Brené Brown, *Daring Greatly: How the Courage to Be Vulnerable Transforms the Way We Live, Love, Parent, and Lead* (New York: Avery, 2015).

cope or survive, which means that coming back into contact with emotions can feel activating to the nervous system as it has been operating under the assumption that emotions are dangerous. This, again, is why it's important to move slowly into this work and to recognize the interconnectedness of the healing process.

Emotions are pieces of information, not facts. However, when individuals are reintroduced to their emotions, people often move from not feeling anything and operating strictly from their thoughts to being swept up in their emotions. When this happens, it's easy to believe that how we feel is the absolute truth and that anyone who questions our feelings is invalidating and, in some way, harming us.

Though our feelings are important, relying exclusively on our emotions may skew our reality and lead to imbalanced conclusions or create difficulties in life and relationships. As individuals heal from religious trauma, they need safe experiences and relationships to learn how to express emotion, but balance is important. Though our feelings are important, how we feel does not reflect reality 100 percent of the time. Moreover, when our bodies have experienced religious trauma, have been in prolonged survival mode, or endured AREs and faith deconstruction, they received messages through sensation and emotion that helped us survive an overwhelming environment but that are no longer helping us. Therefore, it's important to take our mind, body, emotions, history, environment, and context into consideration.

Emotions are just one piece of information to help us understand what is going on inside us and what we need. Combined with our minds, we can use this information to ask for help, take a break, make changes, and implement more useful coping skills to navigate the situation or relationship we are in. The goal is to eventually find a balance of engaging both our thoughts and our emotions.

To get them familiar with engaging their emotions, I ask my clients: If your emotion (such as sadness) had a voice, what would it say? How would it move? An exercise like this helps my clients recognize that they are feeling something ("I feel sad") rather than being defined by the emotion ("I am sad"). Often this creates space to allow an emotion to pass through them rather than engulfing them. Perhaps this is something you could try too.

Like trauma healing, learning how to interact with our emotions is best suited to slow, manageable expressions, rather than overwhelming cathartic release. When we are not used to having the freedom to express emotions or when we lack experience, any amount of emotion can feel overwhelming. The concept of something being too much or too fast is not limited to trauma or other negative experiences. We can also experience too much of lighter emotions, and those can also feel intolerable to our nervous system. Since emotions are felt in the body, intense release of any emotion may feel so overwhelming that the body shuts down or freezes. Or we may feel raw, unsafe, and exposed—easily wounded by even the slightest unpleasantry. When we move too fast into feeling our emotions, it can lead to an emotional hangover; such emotional releases may leave us feeling exhausted, foggy, lethargic, woozy, and like something is not right. This can be disruptive, and it may take a while to feel normal again.

As I noted earlier, religious trauma is a form of complex trauma that for many people is closely aligned with developmental trauma. Due to this, the healing work almost always includes having to teach ourselves skills and give ourselves experiences that we were not afforded when we were younger. This may mean watching something funny, listening to a favorite song, or engaging in a beloved activity to allow yourself to feel joy, happiness, or satisfaction. Or it may mean setting a timer to allow yourself to feel anxiety, uncertainty, or frustration for a limited time before distracting yourself or engaging in old coping mechanisms. It can look like recognizing when you are emotionally reactive and putting yourself to bed, finding sustenance, or wrapping up in a cozy blanket to feel nurtured and cared for. It is now up to us, as adults, to learn how to be the wise, strong, compassionate caregiver who can create a container for our younger self to be able to feel, express, and attach in a way that was not available before.

Engaging in emotional expression slowly and carefully does not mean that we will always have to engage in this way. But because our emotions have been suppressed, it's important to give ourselves the opportunity to begin again. Going slowly helps our bodies move through stages of emotional development and arrive at a healthier place.

Emotional Pendulum

Many HCRs teach us to deny our emotions and instead pay attention to how others feel. Essentially, we are asked to ensure others' comfort at the expense of our own. In a system that values emotional suppression, it's easier to remain unaware of how we feel and to discard our internal experiences for the sake of others' feelings. When we are working on feeling a spectrum of emotions, it's common to experience a pendulum swing. This may look like believing we are not responsible for how others feel and therefore don't need to pay attention to how our words, actions, and reactions affect others. We may think emotional experiences or responses that differ from ours must be more or less valid. Or we may feel permission to treat others without consideration. It can feel threatening when someone else has a different emotional response or experience than we do. However, this difference leads us to take responsibility for determining how to handle the experience in a way that values both ourselves and others. While we are ultimately responsible only for ourselves and how we feel, we can slow the pendulum swing and find balance by maintaining boundaries appropriate to the relationship, knowing where compromise is possible, and recognizing that others' experiences, emotions, and boundaries are important too.

The ability to regulate emotions will eventually transition into the ability to feel and express a healthy sense of aggression. This can help us honor the experiences we have gone through and to resolve trauma energy that is stuck inside us.[4]

Anger

Anger is an emotion that gets a bad rap even outside of religious contexts. Society does not look kindly on people who express anger, especially when those people live in marginalized bodies. Women and other marginalized folks often live with an unspoken understanding that they need to demonstrate composed and soft behavior, even in the face of injustice and danger, due to oppressive, patriarchal systems. Psychologically speaking, we know that anger is an emotion that, like any other emotion, is a piece of information. Anger is the emotion that helps us understand that something important to us has been violated. It even helps us understand potential action that might need to be taken. I believe that anger is an important emotion to feel, especially when we have suffered abuse, harm, and trauma. Anger lets us know that what happened to us was not okay, and it shows us that we matter and are valuable.

Anger is an emotion, not an action. The reason anger tends to get a bad rap is because of the way people choose to express it. For instance, if a referee made a bad call that negatively affected your favorite sports team, people would not think twice if you yelled at the referees, even calling them a name or two. However, if that anger escalated into physically harming someone, that would be considered inappropriate and illegal.

In trauma terms, anger is most closely associated with the fight response in SNS activation. Though we have talked at length about being able to tune in to our bodies and self-regulate, the goal of trauma healing is not to be constantly calm. In fact, our bodies

4. Anderson, "Living Experience of Healing."

need to have access to these SNS responses when danger comes our way! Having access to our SNS and anger helps us stay safe in the face of danger. The anger we feel in dangerous situations is called healthy aggression. This is the energy that courses through us when we protect ourselves or someone else, set a clear boundary, or say no. This is the energy that allows us to stand up in the face of injustice, to confront those who are treating others with abuse and harm, and to demand change when we see inequality. Healthy aggression is empowering and non-demonstrative, as the goal is not to destroy or harm another person but to keep ourselves and others safe.

Healthy aggression is not something that most of us had access to in an HCR, and as a result many of us experienced boundary violations, harm, and abuse. For children especially, any expression of emotion, autonomy, or voice was often met with harsh punishment until the child eventually learned to silence themselves or channel their emotion into more acceptable behaviors. Being unable to listen to one's body and to determine when something is wrong *or* protect oneself is detrimental to children and can follow them into their adult relationships, where they may accept abusive and harmful behaviors as normal.

HCRs often vilify anger and healthy aggression. These systems have rules and guidelines for what is right and wrong and for how to act, think, and feel. If someone's behavior aligns with what is prescribed as "right" and you don't like it, then you are in the wrong and expressing anger would be considered sinful. Similarly, if someone behaves in the "right" way but it harms you, you are to accept it as right. For example, if you have been told that people wearing blue shirts know best and can do no wrong, then if a person in a blue shirt assaults you or violates a boundary, you are conditioned to believe that this is okay behavior. Even if your body says otherwise, because of the prescribed rules regarding someone in a blue shirt, you will be unable to be angry about how you were treated.

The goal of engaging in healthy aggression as you heal from religious trauma is not to live in a perpetual state of anger, ready to pop off at any moment. Rather, engaging with healthy aggression allows us permission to experience autonomy, protection, and safety that we may never have had access to. And, like other trauma-resolution work, we need to give ourselves experiences where our voice is heard, where we can push back when necessary, and where we can express ourselves. This will allow our bodies to experience something different. Becoming familiar with anger and healthy aggression will show us what we are passionate about, who we value, and how to open the door to feel the full spectrum of emotions.

EMOTIONS COLOR OUR LIVES. They are the essence of our humanity, they can get us in trouble, and they can make our world and relationships richer. I have experienced a lot of pain in my life, and acknowledging it, feeling it, and integrating it into my life has not been an easy or pleasant task. However, tending to my pain grants me access to deep joy and satisfaction. When an individual can feel the intensity of an emotion without becoming overwhelmed by it, they tap into the magic of emotions.

11

Reclaiming Sexuality and Pleasure

IN EARLY ADULTHOOD, my commitment to purity culture was at an all-time high. Though I wanted the lifetime of out-of-this-world sex that was promised if I waited for my future spouse, I felt very little sexual desire because I was suppressing every aspect of my sexuality. One evening I went rollerblading with a guy I had a budding interest in. Being alone with someone was frowned upon, but I reasoned that since we would be in public, we weren't technically alone. However, after rollerblading he invited me to his apartment, where he lived alone, for dinner and a movie. I was excited and skeptical. The thrill of someone being interested in me was electric. Despite knowing that if I told anyone in my HCR what I was doing they would have extreme reservations and would have rebuked me, I accepted the invitation and followed him to his apartment.

When we began to watch the movie, I made sure to sit on the floor while he sat on the couch, but he shifted around in his seat and ended up sitting directly behind me. I was conflicted as I noticed my body starting to buzz—something I had never felt before—and my heart beginning to race when he asked me if I wanted a back rub. I said yes and felt his hands all over my back as my entire body felt waves of pleasure washing over it. I loved the way I felt but also wondered if these feelings meant I was sinning. Looking back now I can see that if I had been open to it or had less-rigid boundaries, he would have liked to offer more than a back rub.

I rushed to my car the moment the movie ended, confused about what happened as waves of disgust and shame rolled in. When I got home, I immediately took a shower and scrubbed my body so hard it was red and raw. I wanted to wash off the experience—both the pleasure and the shame.

The number of people leaving church in recent years is difficult to ignore, and media outlets and religious leaders offer different explanations for why it's happening. Rather than looking inward toward the patriarchal, oppressive, and capitalistic nature of HCRs, some pastors claim that people are leaving because they were never actually true believers or because they want to sin—specifically, sin sexually.

Human Sexuality

Individuals are born as sexual beings—even those who identify as asexual. Having inherent sexuality encompasses biological, physical, emotional, relational, erotic, and spiritual feelings and behaviors. These aspects of sexuality include sexual activity and orientation as well as bonds of love, trust, and care between people, spiritual connections, and pleasure. Different aspects of sexuality can affect reproduction and the sexual-response cycle. Sexuality also affects and is affected by the political, religious, cultural, and philosophical aspects of our lives.

If our innate sexuality is all-encompassing—that is, if there is no aspect of the human experience that it does not touch—it becomes an important and powerful tool to connect to ourselves and others. It stands to reason, then, that one way to control other people could be to vilify sexuality and to script rules about how it's expressed. I believe this is why HCRs place so much focus on sins of the body and on sexuality: to control this aspect of someone is to control them entirely. This control comes in the form of creating rules about our bodies, sexuality, and relationships under the guise of offering the holiest, most godly, or most scriptural way to navigate these areas.

In American evangelicalism, these rules are wrapped up in purity culture, and many other HCRs have their own version of this. Purity cultures seek to prescribe behavior, thoughts, and interactions to make oneself pure while suggesting that behaviors, thoughts, and actions outside their prescription are sinful, fleshly, and dangerous. Though human sexuality touches every aspect of life, religious groups often speak of it only regarding sexual interactions with others, human reproduction, and pleasure. This reductionistic view of sexuality is used to drive political policy and to form stances on social and human-rights issues. This view also refuses to acknowledge a person's humanity.

Pleasure

Many HCRs vilify pleasure in addition to vilifying sexuality. Though pleasure is most closely associated with sexual activity, HCRs often frown on pleasure of any kind, including feelings of happiness, satisfaction, and enjoyment, and the feeling one gets when they receive something good or much wanted. It may seem confusing that, given these definitions, HCRs encourage people to avoid pleasure. However, many HCRs think of pleasure as idolatry. The experience of pleasure, both sexual and nonsexual, has an individualistic quality to it. While the pursuit of pleasure, taken to an extreme, can get in the way of other human experiences and emotions and lean toward self-absorption, the individualism

I am referring to involves recognizing that our own experiences, desires, wants, and needs are important and valuable. In this way, pleasure simply for the sake of pleasure is important and can add color to our lives.

However, in HCRs, suffering is often valued over pleasure, and praise is given to those who experience hardship. They are told that they will be persecuted for being a true believer and that life on earth should and will be hard as a result. The opposite of this is pleasure—something that immature and insincere people strive toward. Additionally, since pleasure is experienced in the body, accompanying feelings of deep satisfaction and goodness are seen as feeling good within oneself versus finding worth and value in God. Therefore, pleasure is not prioritized, and any pleasure experienced because of something external should be both short-lived and credited to God.

Purity Culture as Sexual Abuse

I believe that purity culture is a form of sexual abuse. Purity culture seeks to undermine a person's inherent nature, vilify it, disconnect them from it, and outsource their trust and decision-making to others. And like other forms of sexual abuse, purity culture teachings and lifestyles can result in trauma. Anecdotal research is beginning to note that people coming out of purity culture often have the same symptoms as victims of sexual assault. Tina Schermer Sellers noticed this trend in the early 2000s, when she taught a sexuality class at a Bible college. Her students were tasked with writing about their sexuality, and she started to see themes of shame, fear around sex, and PTSD-like symptoms in their writing.[1]

As a clinician, I have seen this phenomenon in many of my clients who have grown up in purity culture. Linda Kay Klein's book

---

1. Tina Schermer Sellers, *Sex, God, and the Conservative Church: Erasing Shame from Sexual Intimacy* (New York: Routledge, 2017).

features many women coming out of purity culture who dealt with symptoms characteristically prominent in sexual assault survivors,[2] and this topic is regularly discussed in consultation groups among the practitioners at the Center for Trauma Resolution and Recovery. Despite many people having cognitively left behind purity culture teachings, the embodied messages of purity culture are very much alive.

Earlier I used the analogy of a dimmer switch versus an on/off light switch to discuss grief regarding the lost process of sexual development. When an individual is not afforded the opportunity to awaken to their inherent sexuality in an age-appropriate way—whether because of sexual abuse or oppressive and controlling messaging—their body can experience later sexual activity as too much, too fast, too soon. The body can be overwhelmed even if that sexual activity is engaged in at the right time according to their religion. This can lead to many physiological and psychological symptoms that survivors of sexual abuse also experience. These may include PTSD, depression, OCD, increased shame, development of autoimmune disorders and gastrointestinal issues, social anxieties and phobia, relational struggles, sexual dysfunction, difficulty implementing boundaries and feeling empowered, fear around engaging in sexual experiences, hyper- or hypo-sexuality, and a feeling of being contaminated.[3]

My research indicates that people feel significant shame and disgust regarding pleasure, specifically bodily and sexual pleasure, and that these feelings are tied to the abusive messaging they heard from HCRs and purity culture.[4] I noticed two main themes in people's journeys to reclaim sexuality and pleasure: (1) resolving trauma from purity culture messaging or other sexualized violence

2. Linda Kay Klein, *Pure: Inside the Evangelical Movement That Shamed a Generation of Young Women and How I Broke Free* (New York: Atria, 2018).
3. Laura E. Anderson, "The Living Experience of Healing the Sexually Traumatized Self" (PhD diss., Saybrook University, 2021), ProQuest (No. 28644488).
4. Anderson, "Living Experience of Healing."

and (2) building confidence to engage with sexuality in a way that felt congruent, safe, and pleasurable to the individual.[5]

Research has found that reclaiming your sexuality goes beyond being able to physically engage in sexual activities. It includes embodiment, which means being able to use your voice, feel empowered, and experience pleasure.[6] Additionally, reclaiming your sexuality also includes sexual health, which goes far beyond absence of disease/infection or dysfunction to include physical, emotional, mental, and social well-being while prioritizing consent, respect, and pleasure.[7] Due to the interpersonal nature of trauma, individuals often become disembodied as a way to keep themselves safe, despite it weakening their sense of autonomy and agency.[8]

Living in a Healing Sexual Body

As I mentioned earlier, many pastors, religious leaders, and parishioners believe that the reason people leave religion is to have sex. Though having sex is often low on the list of reasons why people leave religion, engaging in sexual activity and pleasure is something many rush into or feel pressure to rush into after leaving an HCR. Some people who decide to engage in sexual activity after deconstruction or deconversion experience few adverse effects. But many experience guilt, shame, fear, anxiety, disgust, and physical conditions such as vaginismus or the inability to get or

---

5. Anderson, "Living Experience of Healing."

6. Anderson, "Living Experience of Healing"; Meredith E. Bagwell-Grey, "Women's Healing Journey from Intimate Partner Violence: Establishing Positive Sexuality," *Qualitative Health Research* 29, no. 6 (2019): 779–95, https://doi.org/10.1177/1049732318804302; Heather L. Jacobson et al., "Religious Beliefs and Experiences of the Body: An Extension of the Developmental Theory of Embodiment," *Mental Health, Religion, and Culture* 19, no. 1 (2016): 52–67, https://doi.org/10.1080/13674676.2015.1115473.

7. Bagwell-Grey, "Women's Healing Journey."

8. Anderson, "Living Experience of Healing"; Judith Herman, *Trauma and Recovery: The Aftermath of Violence—From Domestic Abuse to Political Terror* (New York: Basic Books, 1992); Hillary L. McBride and Janelle L. Kwee, *Embodiment and Eating Disorders: Theory, Research, Prevention, and Treatment* (New York: Routledge, 2018).

maintain an erection. These conditions can feel deeply distressing and can lead to other mental and physical health issues. These are some of the symptoms experienced by both survivors of sexual assault and individuals who grew up in purity culture.

Regarding sexuality, what does it look like to live in a healing body after religious trauma? It almost always begins by deconstructing messages you received about the sinfulness of sexuality and tuning in to the natural needs and impulses of your body. Many HCRs teach that sexuality is both natural and sinful, and they instruct one not to give in to sexual arousal or desire until marriage—and then only with one's spouse. Unsurprisingly, while HCRs categorize sinfulness as inherent, they fail to teach that sins such as murder or robbery should be equally as difficult to resist as sexual sins. According to this reductionistic view, living as a sexual being is on the same level with illegal actions that cause extreme harm. A healthier perspective would understand that to resist expressions of human sexuality and sexual desire may actually be to resist God's good design for human beings.

Like other themes in this book, exploring sexuality and experiencing pleasure require more than a cognitive shift in believing that they are natural and human. Exploring sexuality and pleasure is often a slow process that requires resolving how old messages are living in the body and building capacity for new beliefs and experiences. When pleasure and sexuality have been denied, suppressed, and vilified, it can be overwhelming to jump into expressions of them.

HCRs think of the body and sexuality as synonymous, just as they think of sexual expression and pleasure as synonymous. Since engaging with sexuality in a new way can initially feel overwhelming, I encourage people to begin engaging with their bodies and pleasure in nonsexual ways. For safer ways to begin engaging with your body, you might return to chapter 6. Since HCRs don't distinguish between pleasure and sex, you might find that even considering nonsexual pleasure feels activating, in which case, prioritizing embodiment is a great place to start.

When you're ready to engage with nonsexual pleasure, an easy way to do this is by using one or more of your senses. Is there a scent you feel drawn to? A noise or sound? An image, a taste, or a feeling? Pick one sense and engage with it. I love the smell of freshly cut grass, so after the person who mows my lawn leaves, I sit outside for a few minutes and take in the smell; I inhale it deeply, and typically in a few moments I notice a smile creeping onto my face, my chest expands and feels lighter, and I feel a sense of deep satisfaction. To me, that is pleasure. What happens when you use your senses to find pleasure?

Remember, when we are not used to being allowed to feel pleasure, even nonsexual pleasure, an exercise like this might produce anxiety after a few moments. If that happens, that's okay—just take note of how long you can sit with that feeling of pleasure before the anxiety becomes too much. When you do this activity a second time, see if you can sit with the feelings just a couple seconds longer. Once your body begins to learn that feeling pleasure is safe, you can add other sensorial items and notice how your body responds to them.

When you're ready to experiment with sexual pleasure, consider starting small again. For some people it may feel safer to do this with a partner; for others, doing this by yourself will be key. Start by choosing a sense. For the purpose of this example, we will use the sense of touch. Using your hand, lightly touch various parts of your body. I recommend beginning with body parts that are not sexual organs. Notice what it feels like to have your fingers run over your arms or legs, the nape of your neck, the inside of your elbow. Are there any parts that feel better or worse than others? With the parts that feel better or perhaps even arousing, notice if it would be okay to keep your touch in that spot. Experiment with a firmer or lighter touch and see how long you can stay with this sensation before you begin to feel shame, anxiety, or disgust.

Again, take note of this and see if you can stick with it for a few moments longer the next time you engage in this exercise. Living in a healing body offers you the possibility of continuing to expand your capacity for pleasure and viewing your sexuality as a vital and natural part of yourself that should be celebrated.

Real-Life Examples

Haruto is a newly married man who deconstructed from his fundamentalist religion with his partner after they got married. Both grew up in churches steeped in purity culture, and they waited to have sex until they were married. On their wedding night, after having sex for the first time, Haruto locked himself in the bathroom for hours and had multiple panic attacks as waves of shame rolled over him. When his new wife finally coaxed him into telling her what was wrong, he shared that while he enjoyed what they had done together, he felt like an out-of-control sexual animal who had defiled her. While he knew that he was allowed to have sex now that he was married, he could not shake off the messages that sex was dirty and that he had somehow violated his wife. Haruto began the journey to reclaim his sexuality and allow himself to experience pleasure by understanding how these messages were living in his body, by working with the parts of himself that felt activated when he thought about sex, and by learning to experience pleasure in small but manageable doses.

Shantal did not grow up in an HCR but joined in late adolescence after experiencing significant abuse and neglect in her family of origin. Shantal met her husband, Rick, who had grown up in a fundamentalist religion, at her church's young adult group, and they hit it off. Within six months they were married and, despite neither of them having sexual experiences outside of marriage, Shantal knew something was wrong. After a couple years, Shantal felt so much shame about their sex life that she looked for excuses to not have sex with her husband. This alarmed Rick, and he sought out the support of a pastor, who informed the couple that Shantal should confess her sins and ask her husband for forgiveness for not meeting his sexual needs. Shantal submitted to this advice but couldn't shake the increasing feelings of shame and violation.

Secretly, Shantal began seeing a therapist who was not affiliated with the church. After Shantal described her experiences, her therapist compassionately shared with her that what she was describing was nonconsensual sex and assault. Though Shantal could not bring herself to believe that Rick was intentionally doing this, she couldn't deny that what her therapist shared helped her contextualize what had been happening. Shantal and Rick began seeing a couples therapist who understood HCRs and how their teachings could impact sexual relationships. Shantal and Rick focused on rebuilding trust, experiencing pleasure in nonsexual situations, finding safety together, repairing the ruptures that had occurred, and slowly reintroducing sexual pleasure in ways that were consensual and safe.

Kate grew up believing that the first and only man she would ever kiss would be her future husband. Despite not having interest in boys in high school and feeling like she was different, she chalked these feelings up to her faith and continued to dream and plan for the day that God would bring her husband into her life. After college, she and her best friend traveled for six months, and Kate was introduced to cultures and beliefs she had never known about, which caused her to begin to deconstruct her own. Instead of returning to her family's home, Kate opted to take a job in one of the cities she had passed through. By then she was confident that she no longer held the same beliefs as her parents, and she realized that she was starting to make different choices.

At a pub one night she noticed a woman trying to get her attention, beckoning her to play darts. Kate accepted and found herself experiencing feelings for the woman that she had never experienced for any man. As Kate reflected on this experience in therapy, she wondered aloud if she was not straight—if the reason she had been praying for a husband was because she assumed that she was only ever allowed to marry a man. Through her time in therapy, Kate discovered that she was not sexually attracted to men and embraced her sexual orientation as a lesbian. Though she experienced some fear and hesitancy when she began dating women, she had already begun to recognize what pleasure and safety felt like in her body and used that as a guide to determine who and what was important to her.

Reclaiming Sexuality for LGBTQ+ Folks

HCRs have strict rules around gender and sexuality. Purity culture teaches that being anything other than cisgender and heterosexual is a sin. Those who experience same-sex attraction and gender dysphoria or who do not subscribe to a binary system of gender are told they are not allowed to act on these sinful urges; in some cases, their very existence is denied. HCRs often subscribe to extreme practices that further harm, such as conversion therapy, and abusive messaging that often results in lifelong effects.

The exercises I provide throughout this book can be helpful for individuals in the LGBTQ+ community. But those in this community often need to do additional work, such as working through internalized homophobia or transphobia, working through extra layers of shame about their "unnatural existence," and working through fears of being disregarded or disowned from communities, family, and friends. This work can often feel so insurmountable that the very idea of reclaiming sexuality and pleasure may feel out of reach or simply not worth it.

My heart breaks for the many individuals who have been shamed into silence, ridiculed for being different, or required to "be normal," all in the name of God. I am heartened to see churches and religious groups affirming LGBTQ+ people and actively looking for ways to help those who have been harmed, but there is still so much hurt and pain. As religious trauma is continuing to be recognized as trauma, I hope that those in the LGBTQ+ community can find ways to feel supported and can find people to walk alongside them as they heal from the unique ways that they've been harmed. I am extremely grateful for the relationship I have with those in the LGBTQ+ community and for their willingness to share with me some of the important parts of reclaiming their sexuality and pleasure. Here is what they said:

- "Finding other people who had similar experiences to me was so helpful. It was nice to talk to and make friends with people who knew what it was like to have to deny this huge part of who they are because God said so."
- "I realized how much shame I carried for just being me. Learning how to release that shame felt like I lost a hundred pounds overnight."
- "The LGBTQ+ community has a stereotype that all we do is have sex, talk about sex, and think about sex. I had to learn that my queerness is both a gift and only one part of who I am—there is so much more to me than my sexuality. When I let that be a part of me rather than defining all of me, I was able to find so much satisfaction in who I am, my relationships, and my life."
- "I made a point to find a mentor who understood developmental psychology and relationships and who was a part of the LGBTQ+ community themselves (and had been out and proud for decades). It was important to me to learn healthy relationship dynamics and communication, sexual development (since I missed out on everything!), boundaries, and tuning in to my body. It felt like I was launching into the world all over again, just like after high school, but this time it was me as my true self."

These snippets do not capture the magnitude of confusion and pain that many of my friends and clients have experienced. But these quotations give us a glimpse of the moments of lightness and ease that were felt as these people healed from the effects of HCR. Unequivocally, each person I spoke to wanted to reiterate some form of the same message: You matter. You are loved. There is nothing wrong with you; you can trust yourself and who you are. You have people on your side. It won't always be this hard.

Developing a Sexual Ethic

Finally, reclaiming your sexuality and pleasure often requires developing a new sexual ethic for you to live by that feels authentic to who you are. I am careful to not use the phrase "sexual boundaries" in a context like this because in HCRs many people were taught to think of sexual boundaries as lists of things you could and could not do. Conversely, an ethic is a moral philosophy that you choose to live your life by that not only fits who you are right now but can also shift to fit who you are in the future. This is the harder way; it's much easier to have a fixed list of what's good or bad, right or wrong. It's more complex to reflect on your sexuality, how it is expressed, what is important to you, and how that might operate in your life. To be sure, the concept of boundaries discussed in chapter 8 can work in this area as well; understanding what we need to feel safe is also important in sexuality. However, I believe that given the vastness of our sexuality, we would limit ourselves if we discussed only boundaries and didn't consider forming a broader sexual ethic.

What does your sexuality mean to you? What does it mean for you to be female, male, or nonbinary? How does this influence the way you navigate through the world and relationships? How does the outside world influence your sexuality, and how does your sexuality influence the world around you? What aspects of your sexuality are you more comfortable with? What aspects are you less comfortable with? What parts of your sexuality feel unfamiliar? How is your sexuality expressed in romantic and non-romantic relationships? What does sex or being sexually active mean to you—that is, why do you have sex? How do you know you feel safe (e.g., physically and emotionally) to engage in sexual activity? How do you know if you are consenting? How do you know if others are consenting? What do you want to get out of sexual experiences, and is it okay if you don't receive that or if your partner(s) don't want the same thing? How would you know if the sexual ethic you live by no longer fits and it's time to reevaluate?

These are a lot of questions, and yet they are just the tip of the iceberg when it comes to reclaiming our sexuality. The pendulum analogy discussed previously works here too. When coming out of an HCR where sexuality is oppressed and vilified, it can be easy and even natural to swing to the other side of the pendulum to make up for lost time by engaging in lots of sexual activities with or without a partner(s), without inhibition, and maybe even with some risk. While I firmly believe that each person should be allowed to express their sexuality in a way that is authentic to them, so long as they are not harming other people, I also recognize that neither side of this pendulum prioritizes a sexual ethic that is uniquely yours. Why? Because on one side of the pendulum your sexuality is prescribed by someone else and on the other side you are simply doing the opposite of what was prescribed, often in an attempt to feel liberated. Neither side requires thinking about or reflecting on your unique personhood, character, and values. In encouraging you to reclaim your sexuality and pleasure, I am continuing the theme in this book by encouraging you to make your sexuality authentically yours.

12

Establishing Healthy Connections and Relationships with Others

I CAN'T REMEMBER any point in my life when relationships were not central. As the oldest of four siblings, playing with neighbors, making friends at school, being surrounded by hundreds of people every week while living at a camp, working in ministry, and now working as a therapist, coach, supervisor, director, family member, friend, and dog-mom—relationships have always been a key element in my identity. I learned early on that my job was to serve others, and as long as others were comfortable and happy, I could breathe a sigh of relief.

Learning more about how womanhood is depicted in the Bible enhanced my propensity for self-forgetfulness as I leaned in to my role as a submissive helper. I was taught that although my husband would ultimately be the man I would submit to, until he came along, I could refine my skills of submission by practicing on other men in my life. I learned to set my wants, needs, and desires aside even more, to silence and doubt myself, to fragment the parts of me that were "too much" and not characteristic of a quiet and peaceable woman.

I was the poster child for the common acronym JOY: Jesus first, others second, yourself last. In my twenties this looked like being paid for only half the hours I worked at the church. The other half were a way I "tithed" my time. The relationships I had were with people I served alongside or mentored. Even when I wasn't working in a formal ministry position, the people I called friends would drift into my life when they were romantically interested in a sibling of mine and then drift back out if my sibling(s) started dating someone else. I desperately desired relationships where I was being invested in or where my needs mattered, and I prayed fervently for a godly husband. Any expression of frustration or confusion about why my husband had not yet appeared was met with admonishment that I wasn't being patient enough and that I was idolizing relationships.

Even after I began to deconstruct my religion, my relationships continued to have these dynamics. I was friends with people because it was convenient for them and because I could do something for them. I truly appreciated being someone whom others trusted and felt supported by. But it was painful when people left my life because I wasn't living the way they wanted me to or showing up in the way that made them comfortable or because I had needs, wants, and preferences that were "too much." Eventually I began to isolate myself from others as the pain of being hurt in these relationships felt more unmanageable than the pain of being alone.

Relationships inside HCRs

The foundation of HCRs is relationship: relationship to and with God and relationship with others. These religious systems understand our human need for relationship and centralize it in how they appeal to and maintain their group membership. Many HCRs do not advertise their rigid beliefs and practices or use them as reasons you should join their group. Instead, they paint pictures of the built-in community that you will have and how this community mirrors heaven. In most groups, community goes far beyond Sunday morning church services and extends into small groups, accountability groups, playdates, friendships, and romantic partnerships. In some cases these groups encourage members to use fellow group members for their daily needs, such as haircuts, car repairs, legal counsel, and more. For some, this leads to what they consider an enriching and fulfilling life. For others, however, the expectations of group involvement create exhaustion and isolation as members of the group are required to give constantly and tirelessly without pay, rest, or consideration for other commitments.

Anecdotal evidence suggests that the largest group of people who are leaving evangelicalism are not those who were mildly involved or nominal believers. Instead, the people leaving are among the most committed—those who studied the holy texts; served others tirelessly; gave at the expense of themselves, their families, and their well-being; and shaped their lives around the mission of the church. People leaving these religions altogether are often left feeling disillusioned not only with the religious system but also with the people at the top of these hierarchical structures and those they "did life with" day to day.

Beneath the facade of smiling, happy people is a more sinister recognition: group membership is based on being similar in all ways, and difference is viewed as dangerous. Fundamentalism is not exclusive to religion and while many nonreligious groups promote a sense of sameness to inspire group camaraderie, what sets HCRs apart are the consequences, including fears around eternal consequences, for not following the group's rules, standards, and preferences exactly. Rules for life and relationship leave no room for nuance and instead require prescriptive templates for being true believers. Behind the passion for evangelism, a missional mindset, and community outreach are often capitalistic business models that use the idea of working for God's glory to lay claim to people's time, energy, finances, and other resources. Questioning these practices or mentalities leads to the consequences that hurt people the most: the loss of relationship. Many people who have left an HCR lament about the community they lost and the sense of betrayal they feel from those closest to them. They wonder how to find community again—especially community that won't feel exploitative.

In HCRs individuals who are a part of marginalized groups are especially aware that their connection to the group and to individual people often hinges on whether they are willing to make others comfortable. As we discussed in chapter 3, patriarchal systems have an ingrained hierarchy designating which bodies and identities have power and which do not. This hierarchy indicates how much effort one must put forth to gain approval from the group in power. Post-religious spaces on social media contain stories of many individuals of color and disabled bodies who have been tokenized and dismissed. Individuals in marginalized groups often face microaggressions and overt aggression, and yet they are expected to smile and keep silent so as not to disrupt the picture that those in power want to portray.

On top of this, many people inside HCRs were taught that they needed to depend only on God to meet their needs and needed to trust that whatever God was doing was for their own good. An excerpt from my research reads:

> I have been abandoned by a lot of people—I've been used by a lot of people. My desire to be in a committed relationship always seemed to be devastated—hopes were often crushed. It seemed like punishment for various reasons—whether for past sins or "making an idol" out of a person or desire. But the only hope I had to cling to was that God punished those he loved. So, all of the things he seemed to be taking away from me, as a form of disciplining me for whatever he wanted, were actually because he loved me, knew

what was best for me, and had something different in store. And if God was taking the time to punish me—which meant he loved me—it meant that he was there and paying attention to me. He had not abandoned me. So being punished meant I wouldn't be abandoned.[1]

Despite the importance of relationships for healing from trauma, the individual coming out of an HCR often faces unique struggles that those who have survived other trauma may not need to work through. After reading about relationships in HCRs or reflecting on your own or others' experiences, it may seem clear that these types of relational dynamics are flawed. But they are uniquely difficult to heal from because they are built to mirror the version of God that an individual has been taught to believe in.

Many HCRs teach a version of God that is better characterized as a perpetrator of domestic violence. I came to realize what an abusive version of God I had been taught when I was unable to determine who told me what—God or my abusive partner. The God I had been taught about was all loving but also seemed to have no problem drowning the inhabitants of the earth, confusing people's languages, or allowing nations to be raped, pillaged, and destroyed when the people did not follow him the way he wanted.

The Old Testament is based on the Israelites being God's chosen people. The actions listed above were carried out against surrounding nations—those that weren't the chosen nation. This sends an underlying message that it's okay to commit atrocities against people if they aren't part of the chosen group. This translates to individual churches, denominations, and groups using their relational power and authority to abandon, betray, exploit, or punish those who do not relate to them in the way they have determined is *the* way they want to be followed and related to.

1. Laura E. Anderson, "The Living Experience of Healing the Sexually Traumatized Self" (PhD diss., Saybrook University, 2021), ProQuest (No. 28644488).

Therefore, rebuilding healthy relationships and connections with yourself (which has been the focus of much of this book) and others (which is the remainder of this chapter) is important.

Functionally Dysfunctional Relationships

When I work with clients who are hoping to build healthy relationships and connections, one of the first areas we begin working through is what relationships have been like in the past. This often requires brutal honesty about their family of origin, the way they learned to relate to others, and the role they played in relationships; it also requires identifying what worked and did not work in past relationships. Relationships in the context of HCRs have some toxic dynamics by nature. And yet after leaving HCRs, it is not uncommon for people to gravitate toward individuals and groups that have a similar dynamic. This is not because the person is a glutton for punishment; rather, it's because as humans we gravitate toward what is familiar, even if it is not always in our best interest.

I call this functional dysfunction. The idea is that even if something is dysfunctional, if it's familiar to you, it often feels functional. If you are used to being in relationships where you have to set your needs aside, then it will be easier to engage in other relationships like this, even if you have left the environment where these habits developed. A practice of curiosity may include recognizing if you've been in relationships with individuals who are essentially the same person with a different face. You might also take note of what qualities you were drawn to, including how the relationship benefited you or felt familiar to you.

When people leave religion and form different communities, old relational dynamics often repeat themselves. It is not uncommon that people are deemed unsafe if they hold a different position, vote for a different political candidate, or do not place as much emphasis or value on a social cause as others in the group do. People are often expected to use social media platforms as a way to show what they are for or against. They may be told that others are watching what they're posting to determine if they have truly deconstructed their religion, if they're a true ally, or if they're a safe person. In such communities, relationships are still built on fundamentalism, proselytizing, and making converts, just with a different goal. It's common for the pendulum to swing the other way in this area as well: people move from over-giving, over-serving, and losing themselves to self-gratification and fierce individualism. This pendulum swing can feel helpful and necessary for some. Yet in both cases the group insists that their reality or truth is *the* reality or truth. We can see, again, that neither side of the pendulum leads to equal and healthy relationships.

It's important to become familiar with relationship dynamics in HCRs and to examine them collectively (such as within post-religious communities and spaces) and personally. Doing so will help us understand the role that we have typically played and what happens inside our bodies as we engage with new people. It's important to notice who we feel safe with and what biases we have. Are our relationships built on a sense of respect, freedom to show up authentically, and care for one another's humanity despite differences? Or is our safety built on sameness, on aligning ourselves with the loudest voice or the most charismatic person? Do we find ourselves having to dip into old ways of thinking and relating to others in order to be accepted, to calm our anxieties, or to avoid real or perceived threat?

After leaving religion, I found that I still struggled to relate to and trust women—especially women in positions of leadership in their communities or careers—because of the way I had been treated by these types of women in the church and because of the underlying beliefs I had about women in leadership. This greatly impacted my ability to form friendships with other women and was something I needed to resolve and heal from.

It's necessary for white folks to examine how they relate to people of color or to evaluate where they have racial diversity in their relationships. It's necessary for heterosexual and cisgender folks to examine how they relate to folks in the LGBTQ+ community. It's important for those socialized as male to reflect on how they relate to those socialized as female. It's necessary for able-bodied individuals to evaluate how they relate to and interact with disabled individuals or folks with chronic illnesses and pain. HCRs teach us ways of relating to others that do not disappear when we leave the group.

Healing through Relationships

As noted throughout this book, healing is not necessarily linear. Many of its themes correlate with and build on each other. In my research, however, I found that while relationships seemed to be one of the most transformative aspects of living in a healing body after trauma, for many people, engaging in relationships felt impossible until other themes discussed in this book had been explored. When a relational past is filled with abuse, abandonment, manipulation, exploitation, rules with severe consequences, and constant fear of rejection from people and a higher power, it can often lead to periods of significant isolation due to feeling unsafe in both public and private settings.[2] When someone is harmed or traumatized in relationship, it can lead to hypervigilance, inflated stress responses, and feeling panicked when interacting with strangers. In turn, this can cause people to believe that others are plotting against them, that minor disagreements are a threat, and that people are generally unsafe.[3]

2. Anderson, "Living Experience of Healing."
3. Anderson, "Living Experience of Healing"; Jonathan E. Sherin and Charles B. Nemeroff, "Post-Traumatic Stress Disorder: The Neurobiological Impact of Psychological Trauma," *Dialogues in Clinical Neuroscience* 13, no. 3 (2011): 263–78, https://doi.org/10.31887/DCNS.2011.13.2/jsherin.

Recent research indicates that trusting and safe relationships are a vital part of healing from trauma, given the interpersonal nature of trauma. However, experiences resulting in trauma can damage an individual's ability to connect interpersonally.[4] In presenting the results of his study on developing a new world-view as a part of healing from trauma, researcher Charles Manda indicated that participants who connected with others who had similar experiences felt a sense of healing through this identification with others.[5] Other researchers found that individuals participating in social activism as part of healing from sexual assault indicated that understanding others' stories as being similar to their own strengthened their self-worth, confidence, and empowerment.[6]

Though connection and support often feel difficult to navigate for religious trauma survivors due to fears of being hurt again, retraumatized, abandoned, or triggered, an individual's access to safe people who support their healing process is directly linked to quicker healing and decreased emotional distress.[7] Additionally, connecting with a community can enable ongoing healing for those who have experienced trauma. One researcher found that

4. Judith Herman, *Trauma and Recovery: The Aftermath of Violence—From Domestic Abuse to Political Terror* (New York: Basic Books, 1992); Carly Malcolm and Richard Golsworthy, "Working Relationally with Clients Who Have Experienced Abuse: Exploring Counselling Psychologists' Experiences Using IPA," *The European Journal of Counselling Psychology* 8, no. 1 (2019): 144–62, https://ejcop.scholasticahq.com/article/17035-working-relationally-with-clients-who-have-experienced-abuse-exploring-counselling-psychologists-experiences-using-ipa.

5. Charles Manda, "Re-authoring Life Narratives of Trauma Survivors: Spiritual Perspective," *HTS Teologiese Studies/Theological Studies* 71, no. 2 (2015): 1–8, https://doi.org/10.4102/hts.v71i2.2621.

6. See, e.g., C. Strauss Swanson, and D. M. Szymanski, "From Pain to Power: An Exploration of Activism, the #MeToo Movement and Healing from Sexual Assault Trauma," *Journal of Counseling Psychology* 67, no. 6 (2020): 653–668, https://doi.org/10.1037/cou0000429.

7. Angela J. Fong et al., "Changes in Social Support Predict Emotional Well-Being in Breast Cancer Survivors," *Psycho-Oncology* 26, no. 5 (2017): 664–71, https://doi.org/10.1002/pon.4064; Herman, *Trauma and Recovery*.

the communal practices of many Latino and Indigenous communities helped individuals and communities heal on a collective and intergenerational level.[8]

Developing healthy relationships and connections builds on the themes of embodiment, self-trust, boundaries, and stabilizing your nervous system. I am not someone who believes you must love yourself before you can be loved by another, as the cliché suggests. However, I do believe that when we have a history of being in an HCR, we often accept treatment from others and hold beliefs about ourselves that are not conducive to healthy relationships. When we are learning to trust ourselves, to practice embodiment, and to know how to access internalized safety and stability, we are better able to find relationships that do not replicate these dynamics of power and control because those dynamics are no longer safe or okay for us.

Earlier I shared that it is often difficult to feel safe in relationships when you have been harmed within them—especially when there are very few, if any, experiences of relationships or influence outside an HCR. It's already been established that surviving these groups usually requires us to live in a constant state of activation in the service of survival. If you reflect on your experiences in these groups and think about what it felt like to be in your body when you were interacting with others, what do you notice? You may feel one of the four trauma responses we have discussed in this book, or perhaps you feel anxiety, agitation, unease, or something else. Regardless, your nervous system learned over time that being in relationship with someone *felt* a certain way.

I've spoken with many women who still feel on guard and ashamed in the presence of men because that is how they were used to feeling when they were part of their religion. When we are used to feeling certain ways in the presence of people inside an

8. Anderson, "Living Experience of Healing"; K. Schultz et al., "Key Roles of Community Connectedness in Healing from Trauma," *Psychology of Violence* 6, no. 1 (2016): 42–48, https://doi.org/10.1037/vio0000025.

HCR it's likely that we will feel the same way, initially, in the presence of people outside the group. To this end, when we work on stabilizing our nervous system, it helps us find a sense of internal safety that we can connect to as we begin to learn how to relate to others. It gives us the possibility of seeing people as potential friends rather than as scary or dangerous.

In chapter 8, I discussed how Brené Brown's "Anatomy of Trust" outlines important components in learning self-trust.[9] Knowing the areas where you struggle to develop trust with yourself may also indicate where it is difficult to develop trust in relationships. It may also directly point to areas where you have experienced relational and attachment wounds. Stabilizing the nervous system and practicing self-trust often helps determine what boundaries we may need to implement.

As we establish relationships with others, especially when those others are also coming out of HCRs and are learning new ways to relate, it's natural to feel defensive if someone places a boundary for their own safety *and* defensive if someone crosses a boundary or does something that makes you feel unsafe. It's easy to slip into old patterns of relating, such as requiring someone to conform to your comfort level, to agree with you fully, or to prioritize you over themselves. This can create ruptures in relationships that feel difficult to repair as most of us are both unpracticed and activated. When this happens, if you have already established ways to return to your body, regain a felt sense of safety, and recognize what is happening for you, then the opportunity to attempt to repair is possible.

Dealing with Difference

Often the capacity to deal with relational differences feels untenable when leaving an HCR. When you are taught that difference

9. Brené Brown, "SuperSoul Sessions: The Anatomy of Trust," video series, November 1, 2015, https://brenebrown.com/videos/anatomy-trust-video/.

equals danger, it can be difficult to stay present and embodied when you are with someone who is different from you or who holds different opinions, values, and beliefs. Many people have very little experience talking to, let alone being in relationship with, someone who holds different beliefs than they do. Differences in preferences, beliefs, values, or actions can cause such an intense inner turmoil that a person's nervous system is activated and moves into a trauma response. Learning how to expand our tolerance for differences is a helpful and important part of healing religious trauma.

Years ago, I used the reality show *The Bachelor* to help me learn how to expand my tolerance for differences in opinions, views, and values. Between the episodes I would surf the many opinion pieces that were written about each episode and notice when I was getting upset, getting anxious, or dissociating. I taught myself to let the discomfort resolve, like riding a wave, while reminding myself that I was safe. Though the show and others' opinions about it were inconsequential, this practice laid a foundation for navigating difference that I could translate into real life.

As you look to live your life in a body that is healing from religious trauma, you might consider that learning how to expand your tolerance for difference opens the possibility of an enriching life with beautiful people who help us grow, challenge us, laugh with us, cry with us, and remind us of our purpose for living.

Getting Out There!

At this point in the chapter, you might feel like what I am suggesting is way too much. That's fair. As with so much of what we have discussed, starting small is often the safest way to learn how to establish healthy relationships and connections.

When a client indicates fear around establishing relationships with other humans, we start with a pet. If you don't have a pet, you could borrow one from a friend, or if it feels safe enough, you could go to an animal shelter and see if you could connect with a stray or rescue animal. And if a pet feels like too much, start with a plant. I am biased, but I think dogs work great for this exercise as they are usually happy to see you, have a short memory when it comes to your bad moods, and love loving you! The goal here is to notice what it's like to be around another living entity—especially one where the likelihood of rejection is very low. So maybe don't start with a cat. (Just kidding!) Here are a few ideas you might consider experimenting with:

- Notice what happens in your body when your pet does something you consider naughty. Do you get angry (fight mode) or anxious because they didn't act perfectly (flight mode), or do you feel unable to engage with them (freeze mode)?
- What is it like to experience your pet continuing to love you even when you have an off day?
- Notice how often you apologize to them for inconveniencing them (fawn mode) even when your comfort is sacrificed. For instance, if you let them sleep with you, do you move them so that you don't fall off the bed, or do you let them stay because you don't want them to get grumpy with you?

Relating to animals is a great way to notice how you relate to other living beings. It can help you learn how you experience love, which may give you information about how you interact with people.

Another way I encourage clients to slowly introduce people into their life in a way that feels safe is to take their computer or a book to a coffee shop and sit for a while to notice what it feels like to be around people without pressure to interact with them. You might notice what you think or what story you tell yourself about people if you make eye contact with them or if you catch them glancing your way. Notice who your gaze is drawn to or what happens internally if someone smiles at you. You might consider repeating this exercise at different places or going to the same place multiple times and noticing who is a "regular" and waves hello, who makes small talk, and who asks the barista for a food or beverage suggestion. Again, we are looking for small but manageable ways to begin connecting with people. The exercise should stretch us but not move us into intolerable feelings.

Finally, consider online spaces and communities. One of the biggest perks of social media and the internet is that you can connect with people and gain information that would not previously have been available to you. There are many networking groups, social groups, and accounts to connect people who have come out of HCRs, who are healing from religious trauma, or who have deconstructed their religion, among other topics. Some of my dearest friends are people I have met in these online spaces, and I am so grateful for them!

A word of caution: beware of common enemy intimacy. That is, beware of engaging in relationships where the only aspect that draws and keeps you together is having a common enemy (this could be a specific person, a religion, an organization, etc.). While having a common enemy can be a natural way for a relationship to start, healthy relationships evolve beyond the common enemy and create depth and breadth of intimacy.

For a couple years after leaving religion and breaking up with my abusive partner, I was isolated by choice. While I could tolerate the presence of a couple people, the anxiety I felt around most people and new places felt untenable. It felt safer to be by myself. Though I didn't think I was a dog person, my mind quickly changed when I saw a photo of a Bichon Frisé/Shih Tzu mix. I got Phoebe when she was exactly eight weeks old, and I used attachment-based parenting methods to train her. She was, and is, the sweetest dog. For the first eighteen months after I got her, my heart physically hurt because of how much I loved her. But I couldn't say those words aloud; I was terrified that if I let myself attach to her and love her, then she would abandon me like so many others had. But her love for me, no matter how prickly I was some days, started to wear me down, until the day came where I finally told her I loved her. She sat in my lap as tears ran down my face; she seemed to know that I needed her to sit there and show me she wasn't leaving.

We were living in a small neighborhood at this time, and in the six months we had lived there I had managed to avoid my neighbors—as people still felt incredibly scary. On a Friday night in the fall, I took Phoebe on her evening walk and when we rounded the corner, I saw a group of neighbors playing cornhole. I intended to walk by quickly, but Phoebe had other ideas. As we neared the neighbors, she began running toward them as they bent down to greet her. They introduced themselves and asked if I watched college football—which is how all good Southerners spend their Saturdays in the fall! When I nodded yes, they insisted that I come over the next day to watch with them, and I found myself agreeing to the invitation. The next day I considered backing out but reasoned that I could make a quick escape to my house if needed. Hesitantly, I knocked on their door and they greeted me as if they had known me for years; staying until midnight felt like no effort. Phoebe, the perfect wing-woman, seemed to know it was time that I make friends with humans. That single day of football turned into dinners, block parties, holiday parties, and friendships with incredible people who only ever loved me for me, who valued me, and who showed up for me day after day. Many of them are still close friends.

When I was writing my dissertation, I wrote poetry for each theme to add a creative element. Poetry was something I hadn't written before, but it flowed easily and seemed to capture the essence of each theme far better than paragraphs of academic writing. I want to share here the poem I wrote for this theme: the move from fearing people to receiving the gift of relationship.

Alone in my home, just me and my dog
Though it's sunny outside, inside there is fog
I cannot go out there; I must stay in

Despite their smiles and laughter
I cannot handle again when
They leave me, betray me, take from me, and go
Abandon me, reject me, and leave me on my own
It's safer here, just me and my dog
At least they can't hurt me; I'm used to the fog

But is this what life is, to hide in plain day?
To avoid all the people, to not go out and play?
Why must I be so scared, why must I run
From all the situations that are supposed to be fun?
I bristle, get nervous, and wonder where I would hide
I cannot go out, it's possible I'll die
It's safer here, to hide in plain day
At least they can't hurt me; it's not necessary to play

Through boldness and courage, I decide to give in
A day of watching football, an invitation
To meet new people, to laugh and connect
Four hours have passed—I haven't died yet
It seems to me I have made a new friend
Someone who likes me and encourages me when
I tell her it's hard to connect and to be
Present with them; it's hard to be me

Through time, effort, and patience my body learned
Some people are safe; they are worthy friends
They could be trusted and counted on
Each time I spent with them was not the end

My living room, my kitchen, my house is a mess
It's okay though, my friends have just left
From a night of fun, of laughter and song
A little sadness comes up because they have gone
But only for a while; tomorrow we have plans
Alone in my home, just me and my dog
I smile and sigh—I look around, there is no fog

13

Integrating the Living Legacy of Trauma

AT THE BEGINNING OF THE COVID-19 PANDEMIC, when no one knew what was going on, I casually scrolled through Twitter for information. I paused on someone's tweet suggesting that if a person had certain resources and didn't use them to help others, then we could not consider ourselves true allies of that group. Their statement sent me into a tailspin. My face grew hot and an old, familiar feeling of shame descended on me, my anxiety began to spike, and I began to question the choices I was making and even my character. I wondered if perhaps I wasn't a true ally and if I needed to disregard my own fear, override my intuition, and act in the way this person suggested. After an hour, I felt like I needed to jump out of my body, and I considered making a drink despite it being only mid-afternoon. Instead, I made an agreement with myself that I could make the drink if I wanted to, but only after I had walked three laps around my neighborhood. I quickly pulled my boots on and headed outside.

As I walked, I tuned in to the feelings of shame that had descended on me, and I asked my body when it had felt like this before. Immediately a scene flashed before my eyes, and I was back at the church where I had worked. I had been told that if I did not believe the tenets of Reformed theology then I wasn't a true Christian and would be fired from my job. The potential danger that could come from refusing to believe was too overwhelming, and my nervous system responded by fawning.

As I began my second lap around the neighborhood, it felt like puzzle pieces were coming together. The statement on Twitter was from someone I respected and trusted, just like I had my boss. The tone of their arguments felt similar, and my body responded by spiraling into familiar feelings of shame. I employed various coping skills that helped me return to a felt sense of safety. I offered myself compassion and validated my response. Unlike in the past, when I would have shamed myself for an "inflated" response to something that I thought I should have been able to easily dismiss, I now reminded myself and my inner child that one of the long-term effects of CPTSD was being triggered. It wasn't a matter of *if* but *when*. I could thank myself for the work I had done to get to the point that, when triggered, I could access many different resources to help me navigate my way back to the present.

HCR's View of Mental Health

Therapy and other wellness fields are gaining traction in mainstream culture and have become widely accepted tools for dealing with trauma and other mental health issues. This was prompted, in part, by the resurgence of the #MeToo movement in 2017, when society was faced with the grim recognition that many people who have experiences of sexualized violence choose not to tell, press charges, or pursue help and instead live in suffering and silence.[1] Shortly thereafter, Emily Joy Allison and River

---

1. Laura E. Anderson, "The Living Experience of Healing the Sexually Traumatized Self" (PhD diss., Saybrook University, 2021), ProQuest (No. 28644488).

(then, Hannah) Paasch shared their own stories of sexualized violence that occurred in religious contexts using the hashtag "ChurchToo," which rocked both religious and secular communities. Prior to this, many HCRs viewed clergy sexual abuse as isolated incidents or as a Catholic problem. Bringing to light the magnitude of what was happening inside churches also brought to light the severe lack of resources for victims and illuminated victims' increased symptoms, mental and physical health issues, and long-term effects, all of which had been largely dismissed or ignored.

Many churches excuse themselves from reporting crimes of sexual violence by claiming to deal with incidents of sexual violence "in house." Further, many churches perpetuate the notion that mental health issues are a result of sin or lack of faith and can be adequately addressed by spiritual disciplines and the notion that engaging in therapy with a practitioner who doesn't share one's faith will surely lead the person away from God. Thus, individuals with mental health issues resulting from clergy sexual abuse or other religious trauma are discouraged from seeking help outside their church. Instead, they are often given counsel requiring them to think of what they are going through as partially a result of their own sinfulness.

Many of the clients I work with share stories of mental health issues they had when they were in an HCR. These issues went untreated and significantly hampered their ability to function in their daily life and to connect to others and to God. They were given many reasons for their "issues," such as unconfessed sin, lack of faith, being tested by God, or having a demon inside them; their religious leaders did not consider seeking professional support or accurate mental health diagnoses. When leaders dismiss the idea of a formal diagnosis, mental health support, or non-sin-based causes for a person's symptoms, people suffer. Such a response exacerbates a person's mental health symptoms and in some cases leads to chronic physical and mental health issues.

Effects of HCRs Resulting in CPTSD

I have heard, witnessed, and experienced an unfortunate number of stories about the detrimental effects of not receiving appropriate mental health care. While some people do find comfort in spiritual practices, these are often used as a sort of Band-Aid for short-term relief rather than addressing the source of a person's struggles. As has been previously discussed, the effects of an HCR can often result in trauma, and if that trauma goes unaddressed it can result in PTSD or CPTSD. As discussed earlier, CPTSD results when a person experiences ongoing, pervasive threat or overwhelm. In some cases, people may experience CPTSD symptoms prior to having left an overwhelming environment. Typically, however, individuals experience ancillary symptoms, such as depression, anxiety, or religious scrupulosity, because of and as a way to cope with the overwhelm. As you know by now, this is how a body functions when it is in survival mode.

The nervous system being stuck on "on" or "off" can lead to several different physical and mental health diagnoses. When the body is in an overwhelming environment, it goes into survival mode to keep the mind and body from feeling the full impact of what is happening. An example of this might be a soldier who is shot in the leg during a battle. Due to adrenaline and other nervous system functions, the soldier may not experience pain or even notice they have been shot until after they have made it to safety. In the same way, religious trauma survivors may not experience the intensity of PTSD, CPTSD, or other diagnoses until their bodies are able to recognize that they are no longer in danger.

In her memoir on recovering from complex trauma, Stephanie Foo shared the surprise she felt when additional diagnoses emerged as she healed.[2] After meeting with a trauma-informed ob-gyn, she learned that her diagnosis of endometriosis had not

2. Stephanie Foo, *What My Bones Know: A Memoir of Healing from Complex Trauma* (New York: Ballantine Books, 2022).

popped up overnight but had likely been there for many years, even decades, but because her body needed to remain braced for danger, the endometriosis simply could not emerge. Healing is a layered process, and as our body is able to soften, new symptoms often emerge that must be addressed and resolved. This may happen for the remainder of our lives.

In chapter 4, we discussed how our nervous system responds to stress, danger, or overwhelm: it employs bursts of chemicals and hormones, and it shifts the way our body functions to survive.[3] When the danger has passed, our systems are designed to return to a sense of day-to-day functioning and to feelings of safety. But under constant or inescapable stress, our nervous system never has a chance to return to a non-activated state.

When the body is stuck on "on" or "off," it becomes imbalanced, resulting in increased anxiety, pulse, blood pressure, startle responses, dissociation, and numbing. Additionally, it alters our stress response; that is, our ability to handle stress decreases. It also increases hypervigilance and decreases the ability to recognize real threats versus perceived or remembered threats.[4] Over time, this can lead to a variety of other illnesses and disorders including heart disease, autoimmune diseases, chronic pain, chronic illness, reproductive difficulty, depression, disordered eating, gastrointestinal and digestive issues, lowered immunity, chronic fatigue, obesity, and mental health issues (including OCD, depression, anxiety, panic disorders, bipolar disorder, dissociative disorders, social anxiety, and relational difficulties).[5] While the process of

3. Jonathan E. Sherin and Charles B. Nemeroff, "Post-Traumatic Stress Disorder: The Neurobiological Impact of Psychological Trauma," *Dialogues in Clinical Neuroscience* 13, no. 3 (2011): 263–78, https://doi.org/10.31887/DCNS.2011.13.2/jsherin.

4. Sherin and Nemeroff, "Post-Traumatic Stress Disorder."

5. Anderson, "Living Experience of Healing"; Janina Fisher, *Healing the Fragmented Selves of Trauma Survivors: Overcoming Internal Self-Alienation* (New York: Routledge, 2016); Peter A. Levine, *In an Unspoken Voice: How the Body Releases Trauma and Restores Goodness* (Berkeley: North Atlantic Books, 2010); "Stress System Malfunction Could Lead to Serious, Life Threatening Disease," National

trauma resolution may reduce or alleviate some of these symptoms, many people find that the result of trauma after HCRs often means learning how to live and even thrive with CPTSD.

Living with CPTSD

Discussing the long-term effects of CPTSD, Judith Herman indicates that the pervasive nature of trauma often leads to enduring disturbances in the areas of the self, affect, and interpersonal relationships.[6] This is not to say that diagnoses of PTSD, CPTSD, or other trauma-related diagnoses are a death sentence. Rather, ongoing healing must happen on multiple levels because trauma impacts us on multiple levels. Further, it means that the themes of healing that have been discussed in this book so far are not only indicators of living in a healing body after religious trauma but also areas to be integrated into the rest of your life for the rest of your life.

Simply put, the person who has been traumatized by religion may sometimes find it easy to engage in relationships or regulate their nervous system and other times find it quite difficult. Sometimes no formal cognitive deconstruction will be going on, and other times more excavation work will be required. The ongoing nature of healing, which includes integrating the themes in this book, becomes the way that we live in and navigate the world.

In my doctoral research and in client sessions, the theme of this chapter seems particularly important. Many individuals who have experienced HCRs and/or AREs may qualify for a diagnosis of PTSD, CPTSD, or another physical or mental health disorder. While neither a self-diagnosis nor formal diagnosis is required to heal from religious trauma, in my experience, a diagnosis can act

Institutes of Health, September 9, 2002, https://www.nichd.nih.gov/newsroom/releases/stress#.

6. Judith Herman, *Trauma and Recovery: The Aftermath of Violence—From Domestic Abuse to Political Terror* (New York: Basic Books, 1992).

as a helpful framework for understanding your experience, what's happening in the present, how to move toward the future, and how the previous themes in this book may show up prior to and after trauma resolution.

Many people who ask someone to support them through their trauma-resolution process do so with the intention that once their trauma is resolved, their lives will go back to normal. Sometimes this is the case. For individuals who have experienced single incident trauma, resolving the trauma can remove some of the effects of those events—especially if someone has resources such as safe relationships and coping skills. However, when an individual does not have access to these resources or has complex trauma, part of healing includes recognizing the way their life is affected for the remainder of their life. This process often includes grieving for the ways their life and body were altered.

Complex trauma survivors often experience moments every day where they face familiar feelings, triggers, or other difficulties related to what they have formerly experienced. When the perceived or remembered feelings and sensations infiltrate, it becomes difficult to stay in the present moment. It's common in these moments to get swept backward—as if you are in the past when the abuse, danger, or overwhelm was taking place. This can involve inflated or deflated reactions disproportionate to the situation in the present moment. This isn't to say that the trauma survivor's goal is to handle all situations in a calm, cool, and collected manner; we have these nervous system responses for a reason. A goal of complex trauma resolution is to be aware of when your nervous system is pulling you into the past and, instead of being swept up into the experience, building the capacity to access different coping skills that promote a felt sense of safety. This will result in having more choices about what you want to do next.

In working with survivors of complex trauma, a word I like to use is "integration." In trauma work, integration is the process of bringing the past into the present. When someone has CPTSD, they have usually experienced many incidences that were distressing and that significantly impact the present. Though not true in all cases, many individuals who have CPTSD can't identify one or two overwhelming moments and instead remember pervasive feelings of danger and unsafety, stress, overwhelm, helplessness, and powerlessness. Trying to process each of these moments in a therapeutic context would be nearly impossible, not only because of the sheer volume but also because many incidents may not be remembered for years, if ever. Instead, we work to develop resources and a sense of internal safety and then bring those skills into daily life.

Making Accommodations

When I was an active participant in religion, I was very rigid with my routine. Every part of my life was built around practicing spiritual disciplines, participating in ministry, and serving others. After leaving religion, I discarded this unyielding routine. In fact, I became quite activated even thinking of having a routine. I eventually realized that my body had connected routine and structure with fear, shame, and guilt. When I stuck to my routine, it meant that my walk with God was going well. But missing an element of my carefully crafted schedule could lead to grave consequences, and not structuring my life around the disciplines of my faith brought on immense amounts of guilt. Anything that resembled the discipline with which I had to live my religious life felt triggering, so I discarded all aspects of structure. Even as I became less activated by this trigger, my life seemed to deteriorate in other areas. I struggled to take care of basic needs, was unable to perform daily tasks and chores, and, despite knowing what I could do to help myself, I felt unable to.

Though it pained me to admit it, I could easily recognize that my religious routine and structure had provided me with a coping mechanism that helped me get through the day-to-day overwhelm of my environment, and I missed it. As I learned to uncouple—that is, to pull apart routine and structure from guilt, shame, and fear—I was able to realize that living in a healing body meant that it was necessary to have a routine without shaming myself. It was essential for me to prioritize this, even if doing so required certain accommodations.

Though the United States is largely ableist, strides have been made in recent decades to make accommodations for individuals with disabilities. Moreover, we recognize that the accommodations are not because someone is weak or inept but because we are all unique and not everything works the same for everyone. Our culture is beginning to embrace disability accommodation and to look for ways to provide an opportunity for people to thrive. This is why when we see an individual using a wheelchair or requesting that a test be read aloud to them, for example, we do not shame them or think of them as incompetent. We recognize that everyone has different needs. Yet we are slower to recognize the disabilities that are not visible to others. When it comes to mental health and trauma, we are not as quick to consider that accommodations may be necessary.

Since trauma can have lifelong effects, it is safe to assume that we may need extra support in some areas of our lives—for a period of time or forever. Just like we would not shame an individual with a broken arm for their arm not healing fast enough, we might consider offering the same amount of compassion and patience to ourselves and others when the lingering effects of trauma do not disappear because we've gone to therapy or done some amazing trauma-resolution work.

When I realized that the impact of trauma was long-lasting and that healing was ongoing, I replaced shame with self-compassion and made small but significant changes that not only made my life easier but also allowed me to feel like I was in control of my life. Many of my clients have had similar experiences. They have recognized that even after trauma is resolved, they still need to make accommodations that help them deal with the enduring impact of trauma. Below are some of the most prevalent accommodations for living with the life-long effects of trauma that I discuss with my clients.

Basic Needs

When a client comes in with high anxiety and stress, one of the first areas I check on is basic needs. Are they getting enough sleep? Enough food? Water? Movement? Connection to humans? In many cases, once basic needs are attended to, my clients find they have a much easier time dealing with life stressors. With my trauma clients, this is even more important and is part of the trauma-recovery process. Each person will be different regarding what they need to function, but prioritizing these in your schedule and life can sometimes be the difference between an easy or a difficult day or season of life. It may take some experimenting to find the right combination for you, and I encourage you to do just that: experiment.

Notice how you feel during the day when you have five to six hours of sleep as opposed to seven to eight. Notice whether snacking between meals helps you stay focused and engaged or whether you function just fine with three meals each day. Digestive issues are common for trauma survivors, which means that paying attention to the foods you eat and the physiological and psychological effect they have on your body will be important. For instance, when I eat foods that have gluten in them, my abdomen distends, I get moody, and I struggle to concentrate. Eating foods that work well for our bodies aids in optimal physical and mental health.

Movement is another need that is essential for the human body—and I'm not even talking about vigorous exercise! Our bodies need opportunities to move throughout the day. This could be through chair yoga, stretching, light walking, or gentle swaying. Individuals who have limitations with movement might consider modifying some of these things: sway your arms, roll your wrists or ankles, gently turn your neck, or use micro-movements and notice other sensations in your body.

Human connection is a basic need, as we have seen from previous chapters discussing attachment theory and establishing healthy relationships. Since social connection can often feel difficult and/or scary, accommodations include scouting out public places before you go there and giving yourself an out in a social interaction, such as needing to go home to take care of your pet, so that you don't become overwhelmed. Unresolved trauma often leads to isolation because it can feel physiologically safer. Relationships and connection, therefore, may require accommodations as you ease back into the world.

Lowered Capacity for Stress

Some of my clients are discouraged by their diminished capacity to handle stressful situations. Many of them look back on the days where they could spin thirty-two plates in the air while hopping on one foot with perfection, and then do it all again the next day. They experience immense shame for being overwhelmed or exhausted by basic or mundane tasks. While most people's capacity for handling stress does increase as they resolve trauma, many people are unable to recover their previous capacities, especially for handling day-to-day stress. One caveat is that while traumatized individuals may struggle to deal with day-to-day stressors, they often seem to be incredibly resilient when the world is falling apart—literally and figuratively.

In March 2020, as the world was beginning to grapple with a global pandemic, I noticed a strange phenomenon among many of my clients and social media followers and even within myself. They displayed a sense of calm while the rest of the world was spiraling. Funny memes began to float around the internet pointing out that while the rest of the world was figuring out how to live while everything was falling apart, individuals with CPTSD were in familiar territory. Trauma survivors know how to plan for catastrophe and how to deal with pervasive overwhelm and anxiety. And for many, the idea of not having to interact with many (or any!) people daily was a break that they had been waiting for. While the pandemic did affect them, many did not experience the frenzy that others felt.

I've reflected on this dynamic since then, and I believe the memes are right. Individuals whose life experiences resulted in trauma and CPTSD have a keen awareness of how to deal with high stress, overwhelm, and conflict. It is familiar territory. All the survival skills that had been necessary to survive earlier parts of their lives were useful, and the big stressors that a pandemic provided seemed not to phase them at all.

Interestingly, the same clients who seemed to sail through the pandemic now express significant distress about the mundane, daily tasks that many other people navigate with ease. As it pertains to a lowered capacity for stress, whether facing a global pandemic or navigating Costco aisles on a weekend, developing self-compassion is key for establishing accommodations in this area. While prioritizing basic needs is essential for lowering stress, even meeting your basic needs can feel exhausting when stress is high. I see this the most with my food intake. When my stress is high, I forget to eat. This then brings on all sorts of physiological and psychological issues, which then increases my already high stress. When stressed, I prioritize foods that are quick and easy, even if they aren't considered the healthiest. In those moments I know that getting calories into my body is more important than ensuring that I am eating the right proportions of each food group.

When our capacity for stress is decreased, many of us need to listen to our bodies more intentionally. Whereas in the past it may have felt relieving to escape from our bodies, disconnecting from or disregarding our bodies means that we don't have valuable information that can help us support ourselves. Accommodations may include intentionally tuning in to our bodies or orienting to the space around us, listening to the needs of our bodies—whether basic needs or needs for boundaries, pleasure, or nervous system regulation—and making the necessary accommodations to ensure that our bodies are getting what they need.

CPTSD Flare-Ups

Individuals with chronic illnesses or pain, autoimmune disorders, or individuals with old injuries are familiar with flare-ups. Flare-ups are times when the illness, pain, or injury reemerges, and special accommodations must be made to deal with what is no longer dormant. Sometimes this includes increasing rest, changing diet, slowing down, or taking medicine. Individuals with chronic conditions learn that flare-ups happen, often with no rhyme or reason, and they must attend to their body and employ coping skills they have learned that will offer relief, even in small amounts.

CPTSD is like this as well. Sometimes it flares up, and then we need to attune to it in a different way, accommodating what our bodies and minds need to gently ride the wave. Many of my clients become confused, angry, or ashamed when this happens. They often feel as though they have done something wrong or that the work they have done is meaningless. In these moments I ask them to borrow the compassion I have for them and apply it to themselves as they begin to understand what is happening. Knowing that CPTSD flare-ups are a matter of when, not if, can help you care for yourself in a patient and kind way.

A CPTSD flare-up can manifest in many of the ways that were present prior to doing trauma-resolution work. Perhaps you become triggered or irritable more quickly, depression or anxiety are constant, relationships feel extra difficult, or self-harming behaviors seem challenging to resist. During these times it may be difficult not to slip back into old survival patterns, believe narratives about the danger of others, or shut down completely. Sometimes flare-ups arise as the result of an anniversary of a particularly overwhelming event, of unmanageable stress, or even of various headlines about events in the world around you.

One of the greatest gifts you can give yourself when flare-ups happen is self-compassion. Understanding that you will almost certainly experience a flare-up at some point and giving yourself space to recognize that this makes sense can create space for you to employ coping mechanisms, find internal safety, and even reach out to others for support and coregulation.

The Living Legacy of Trauma

One of the trauma therapists and educators who has been most influential for me is Janina Fisher. In her most recent book, she discusses what she calls the "living legacy of trauma."[7] A legacy is something that is transmitted from the past. While most think of a legacy as something transmitted from an ancestor or predecessor, a living legacy is something someone received in the past and is now still living with. Fisher's work backs up my research in recognizing that we are living and healing each day. The idea of a living legacy doesn't involve pretending that what happened was okay or that if we survived it, learned from it, or are stronger because of it, it was somehow worth it. The idea of trauma as a living legacy recognizes that what happened was not okay and that even though you are doing the messy, brave, and courageous work of healing, it stinks that you must do it.

In this willingness to look at our trauma accurately and honestly, I see each of the themes of healing come together. Living the legacy of trauma means that sometimes life will be more difficult, and sometimes it will take more effort or attention. But offering compassion to ourselves gives us a shame-free path through the pain. Grieving opens the door to feeling whatever comes up, to

---

7. Janina Fisher, *Transforming the Living Legacy of Trauma: A Workbook for Survivors and Therapists* (Eau Claire, WI: PESI Publishing, 2021).

riding those waves of emotions and sensations to completion so that we can make choices that are congruent with who we are. It means that there may always be new facets we learn about ourselves, our pasts, and the world. We might have to remodel our worldview several times; as we have space from environments that harmed us, we will have room to breathe and to consider new, fresh ideas and integrate them into our lives.

Living the legacy of trauma may mean we have to work harder to form relationships, set boundaries, or show up authentically. It may mean that reclaiming pleasure moves at a snail's pace while we recognize that even incremental progress should be celebrated. And it often means that, like any relationship, the relationship we have with our bodies and nervous systems requires daily, intentional attunement and care.

My Living Legacy

Both diagnoses I have received have been helpful tools in my living legacy. When I reread the journal entries I wrote prior to my diagnoses, I can see persistent confusion because I had symptoms that baffled therapists, healers, and doctors. Despite sharing with various support people what I had endured, no one ever mentioned trauma. I was diagnosed with anxiety, depression, adrenal exhaustion, candida overgrowth, low iron and vitamin D, and social anxieties. As a result, I became more isolated, self-critical, dysregulated, harsh toward myself, and terrified of my own body.

It took six years of visiting various healers and helpers before a therapist helped me recognize that my symptoms matched the diagnoses of CPTSD and dissociative identity disorder, not otherwise specified (DID-NOS). This dissociation disorder is common among survivors of complex trauma. As I revisited my journals to use in my dissertation, I found myself chuckling at the language I used to describe my state: feeling fragmented, feeling internally at war, struggling with relationships, having gastrointestinal issues, being unable to carry out even basic life tasks, and experiencing extreme dissociation. Despite not yet having a diagnosis, I was already living my trauma legacy.

It's been years since those aha moments in my therapist's office. Being able to recognize trauma, CPTSD, and DID-NOS allowed me permission to reflect on my life and my present behaviors through a different lens. Suddenly it all made sense, and as I saw myself through this new lens, I could begin to heal in an active way. I have learned to be patient and tender with the fragmented parts of me that sometimes like to take over when I am scared or overwhelmed. I've learned how to reach out for support—to send a text and honestly share what is happening, even when it feels terrifying. I can feel when my body goes into SNS activation, and I can use medicine and coping skills to help me return to a calm state. I make the accommodations I need in my schedule and routine, my social life, and my relationships. I remind myself that these accommodations allow me to live in the present rather than being held hostage to my past. Trauma is my living legacy. My compassionate embrace of this allows me to create a new path—a new legacy as I venture forward.

Conclusion

AS I WRITE THIS, I am staring down about six months of "trauma-versaries" (the anniversaries of when some really bad stuff happened). Some years I hardly think about it when I reach those anniversaries; other years I think about it a lot. This year feels different. My body is already feeling the toll of what happened in a more acute way. I am forced to slow down, to offer patience and kindness to myself, and to notice where any old, stuck trauma energy is living. I used to get upset because *x* number of years had passed, and I was *still* dealing with the effects of trauma. I desperately wanted to move on and forget about all that had happened.

I used to fear that my life would be characterized by what had happened to me. But now I appreciate my tenacity in working through the hard stuff and moving forward. I no longer fear that my body being more exhausted, being more sensitive, having less bandwidth, or being more prone to being triggered means that I'm stuck in the past. Instead, I view my life experiences as pieces of me that I must accommodate because of the traumatic injuries I have suffered. Instead of shaming myself, I offer myself compassion and gratitude for how far I have come.

This is what healing is all about—the process. Perhaps this year or next year or ten more years down the road my body will no longer respond to trauma-versaries, but that is no longer my goal.

I have lived far too much of my life with the end goal of eternal life in heaven, and so I missed a lot of life on earth. These days, even in the dark, difficult, and painful moments, I let my body take the space that I need to come back home to myself. I give myself many moments to reflect and to celebrate how far I have come. It's astounding, really.

This book is meant to show you what life can be like after being in high-control churches, groups, and relationships; after enduring experiences like AREs and purity culture; and after living a life of fundamentalist rules that dictated every aspect of your identity and that had far-reaching consequences. Just like trauma is subjective to the individual, so is healing. I hope that the themes of healing explored in this book will act as a starting point that you can adapt as needed.

Our unique identities play a role in our healing journey as well. Our identities may make some themes of healing more or less difficult or require more or less effort to pursue. My identity plays a role in how this was written: my professional identity factors in, and the privileges I have or don't have in this world count too. I hope that you can take from this book what you need, leave what you don't, and expand in the ways that feel the most important to you.

I did not aim to create a step-by-step guide of how to heal from religious trauma; rather, I wanted to point out healing themes and to help you learn what it looks like to move from the version of yourself that was altered because of an HCR to a whole and healing version of yourself. That said, many excellent resources and types of support are available to help you continue this journey, depending on what you are looking for and what resources you have (see "Additional Resources" at the end of this book).

As I've written many times throughout this book, start small. It can feel exhilarating to have words to describe your experiences and to feel that you understand what you want to work on by yourself, with your friends, or with a therapist. But it can feel overwhelming too. Choose the smallest and most manageable thing and start there. When I start working with new clients, I tell them, "We will only go as slow or as fast as your nervous system lets us." Usually, it's way slower than they originally anticipated. But what happens, every time, is that when a person is allowed to go at the pace their nervous system needs, they inevitably start to see changes and are then able to move faster. I believe this will be true for you too.

Healing is a lifelong journey with no end point. However, my invitation to you is this: instead of hearing that statement and feeling dread and heaviness, what would it be like to hear it as an invitation to spend each day leaning more into your inherent goodness—the person you were originally created to be before you learned others' versions of who you should be? Sometimes the work of your living legacy will be grueling as you excavate wounded parts of you that have remained hidden in order to protect yourself. Other times the work is filled with lightness and ease as part of the process of living in a healing body includes the actual living. Living in a healing body after religious trauma does not mean that every day or season of your life will need to be spent in therapy, in tears, or feeling held back by the experiences of the past. You will also have moments of celebration as you realize how far you've come, as you inhale the present moment, and as you look around at your brilliant, messy, beautiful self and know that you are free.

APPENDIX

Religious Power and Control Wheel

LOSS OF AUTONOMY
shutting down intuition and personal thought or opinions * inability to trust yourself * needing external authority * all time, resources, energy spent on religious activities * "die to yourself" * must believe, think, act like the group * diverging from the group = tension and excommunication * inability to challenge authority / authority not held accountable * deferring decision-making to spiritual authority * no critical thinking

ISOLATION
cutting off relationships with people outside the system * information control * asking for reporting of where time or money was spent * increased level of commitment to the system's activities * devaluing people not in the religious system * fear/ propaganda regarding motives of people outside the system

MINIMIZING, DENYING, BLAMING
saying the abuse didn't happen * denying the severity of what happened * victim blaming * calling things "sin issues" vs. abuse * requiring forgiveness * taking ownership for how someone else's actions harmed you * downplaying the need for secular support (e.g., police) * denying illegal actions * minimizing felt sense, emotion, or experience * placating statements (e.g., "he's a sinner too, just like you")

SEXUALITY AND GENDER DEFINING
rigid gender roles * inherent sinfulness of specific sexual expressions * gender boundaries * belief in the superiority of one gender over another * patriarchal values * policing of sexual expressions * requirements of purity * punishment for premarital sexual activity * declaring individuals acting outside prescribed gender and relational roles as sinful * suppression of sexuality * blaming the victim for sexual violence * male privilege * referring to God as "he" only, rejecting female spiritual imagery

RELIGIOUS POWER AND CONTROL

EMOTIONAL ABUSE
name calling (e.g., "sinner") * required suppression of parts of yourself * inability to trust yourself * reliance on external authority * fear of consequences for breaking rules * brainwashing/indoctrination * information control * fear of abandonment for nonconforming thoughts or actions * devaluing of body and emotions * coercion * manipulation

ECONOMIC CONTROL
requiring a portion of your paycheck to go to the church * unpaid volunteer hours expected even at the expense of other commitments * devaluing of education (especially for women) * must trust God to provide vs. charity or personal action * inciting guilt over needing to give more time or money to the church * "God will meet all of your needs"

THREATS, ACCUSATIONS, AND INTIMIDATION
threatening abandonment or excommunication for sinning or going outside the group * leaving the church = the devil will try to get you * behavior control * fear of going to hell * accusations that you are going against God * using their position of power to require you to do, say, or believe something * not allowing you to seek external help (e.g., medical, law enforcement)

SPIRITUAL ABUSE
required to submit to spiritual authorities * "God says . . ." * "The Bible says . . ." * no accountability for clergy * decisions made on your behalf or "for your own good" * threatening consequences for breaking group rules/sinning * requiring certain beliefs, thoughts, behaviors with severe consequences for not following * not allowed to ask questions * nonadherence to social rules * use of holy text or position to oppress or abuse

ADDITIONAL RESOURCES

THERE ARE MANY RESOURCES—including low-cost, instant PDF downloads—available at www.drlauraeanderson.com. There is a membership space, Cheaper than Therapy, as well as information on how to get individualized support and guidance.

Please note that although the following resources are incredible and credible, they are not a replacement for a therapeutic or coaching relationship or mental health or medical care. The following books are provided as additional resources and are not necessarily a reflection of my views.

Trauma

Fisher, Janina. *Healing the Fragmented Selves of the Trauma Survivor: Overcoming Internal Self-Alienation*. New York: Routledge, 2017.

Gutiérrez, Natalie Y. *The Pain We Carry: Healing from Complex PTSD for People of Color*. Oakland, CA: New Harbinger, 2022.

Heller, Laurence, and Brad J. Kammer. *The Practical Guide for Healing Developmental Trauma: Using the NeuroAffective Relational Model to Address Adverse Childhood Experiences and Resolve Complex Trauma*. Berkeley: North Atlantic Books, 2022.

Herman, Judith. *Trauma and Recovery: The Aftermath of Violence—From Domestic Abuse to Political Terror*. New York: Basic Books, 1997.

Hübl, Thomas. *Healing Collective Trauma: A Process for Integrating Our Intergenerational and Cultural Wounds*. Boulder, CO: Sounds True, 2020.

Kain, Kathy, and Stephen J. Terrell. *Nurturing Resilience: Helping Clients Move Forward from Developmental Trauma*. Berkeley: North Atlantic Books, 2018.

Levine, Peter. *In an Unspoken Voice: How the Body Releases Trauma and Restores Goodness*. Berkeley: North Atlantic Books, 2010.

———. *Sexual Healing: Transforming the Sacred Wound*. Boulder, CO: Sounds True, 2003. Audiobook, 2 hr., 3 min.

Levine, Peter, and Maggie Kline. *Trauma-Proofing Your Kids: A Parent's Guide for Instilling Confidence, Joy, and Resilience*. Berkeley: North Atlantic Books, 2008.

Maté, Gabor. *When the Body Says No: Exploring the Stress-Disease Connection*. Hoboken, NJ: Wiley, 2003.

Maté, Gabor, with Daniel Maté. *The Myth of Normal: Trauma, Illness & Healing in a Toxic Culture*. New York: Avery, 2022.

Menakem, Resmaa. *My Grandmother's Hands: Racialized Trauma and the Pathway to Mending Our Hearts and Bodies*. Las Vegas: Central Recovery Press, 2017.

Miller, Alice. *The Body Never Lies: The Lingering Effects of Hurtful Parenting*. Translated by Andrew Jenkins. New York: Norton, 2005.

Pasquale, Teresa B. *Sacred Wounds: A Path to Healing from Spiritual Trauma*. St. Louis: Chalice, 2015.

Perry, Bruce, and Oprah Winfrey. *What Happened to You? Conversations on Trauma, Resilience, and Healing*. New York: Flatiron Books, 2021.

Schwartz, Arielle. *The Complex PTSD Workbook: A Mind-Body Approach to Regaining Emotional Control and Becoming Whole*. Berkeley: Althea, 2016.

Van der Kolk, Bessel A. *The Body Keeps the Score: Brain, Mind, and Body in the Healing of Trauma*. New York: Penguin Books, 2015.

Walker, Pete. *Complex PTSD: From Surviving to Thriving*. Lafayette, CA: Azure Coyote, 2013.

Abuse and Dynamics of Power and Control

Allison, Emily Joy. *#ChurchToo: How Purity Culture Upholds Abuse and How to Find Healing*. Minneapolis: Broadleaf Books, 2021.

Baker, Connie A. *Traumatized by Religious Abuse: Helping Survivors Find Courage, Hope and Freedom*. Eugene, OR: Luminare, 2019.

Bluhm, Tiffany. *Prey Tell: Why We Silence Women Who Tell the Truth and How Everyone Can Speak Up*. Grand Rapids: Brazos, 2021.

Blyth, Caroline. *Rape Culture, Purity Culture, and Coercive Control in Teen Girl Bibles*. London: Routledge, 2021.

Ingersoll, Julie. *Evangelical Christian Women: War Stories in the Gender Battles*. New York: New York University Press, 2003.

Johnson, David, and Jeff VanVonderen. *The Subtle Power of Spiritual Abuse: Recognizing and Escaping Spiritual Manipulation and False Spiritual Authority within the Church*. Minneapolis: Bethany House, 1991.

Morris, David. *Lost Faith and Wandering Souls: A Psychology of Disillusionment, Mourning, and the Return of Hope*. Grand Rapids: Lake Drive Books, 2022.

Mullen, Wade. *Something's Not Right: Decoding the Hidden Tactics of Abuse and Freeing Yourself from Its Power*. Carol Stream, IL: Tyndale Momentum, 2020.

Thomas, Shannon. *Healing from Hidden Abuse: A Journey through the Stages of Recovery from Psychological Abuse*. Scottsdale, AZ: MAST, 2016.

Rebuilding a Worldview

Benbow, Candice Marie. *Red Lip Theology: For Church Girls Who've Considered Tithing to the Beauty Supply Store When Sunday Morning Isn't Enough*. New York: Penguin Random House, 2022.

FitzGerald, Frances. *The Evangelicals: The Struggle to Shape America*. New York: Simon & Schuster, 2018.

Garcia, Kevin Miguel. *Bad Theology Kills: Undoing Toxic Beliefs and Reclaiming Your Spiritual Authority*. Self-published, 2020.

Menakem, Resmaa. *The Quaking of America: An Embodied Guide to Navigating Our Nation's Upheaval and Racial Reckoning*. Las Vegas: Central Recovery Press, 2022.

Miller, Alice. *For Your Own Good: Hidden Cruelty in Child-Rearing and the Roots of Violence.* New York: Farrar, Straus and Giroux, 1983.

Onishi, Bradley. *Preparing for War: The Extremist History of White Christian Nationalism—and What Comes Next.* Minneapolis: Broadleaf Books, 2023.

Tarico, Valerie. *Trusting Doubt: A Former Evangelical Looks at Old Beliefs in a New Light.* 2nd ed. Independence, VA: Oracle Institute Press, 2017.

Building a Relationship with Your Body

Caldwell, Christine. *Bodyfulness: Somatic Practices for Presence, Empowerment, and Waking Up in This Life.* Boulder, CO: Shambhala, 2018.

Fay, Deirdre. *Becoming Safely Embodied: A Guide to Organize Your Mind, Body and Heart to Feel Secure in the World.* New York: Morgan James, 2021.

Hornthal, Erica. *Body Aware: Rediscover Your Mind-Body Connection, Stop Feeling Stuck, and Improve Your Mental Health through Simple Movement Practices.* Berkeley: North Atlantic Books, 2022.

McBride, Hillary. *The Wisdom of Your Body: Finding Healing, Wholeness, and Connection through Embodied Living.* Grand Rapids: Brazos, 2021.

Taylor, Sonya Renee. *Your Body Is Not an Apology: The Power of Radical Self-Love.* Oakland, CA: Berrett-Koehler, 2018.

Teng, Tara. *Your Body Is a Revolution: Healing Our Relationships with Our Bodies, Each Other, and the Earth.* Minneapolis: Broadleaf Books, 2023.

The Nervous System

Dana, Deb. *Anchored: How to Befriend Your Nervous System Using Polyvagal Theory.* Boulder, CO: Sounds True, 2021.

———. *Polyvagal Exercises for Safety and Connection: 50 Client-Centered Practices.* New York: Norton, 2020.

———. *The Polyvagal Theory in Therapy: Engaging the Rhythm of Regulation.* New York: Norton, 2018.

Johnson, Kimberly Ann. *Call of the Wild: How We Heal Trauma, Awaken Our Own Power, and Use It for Good.* New York: Harper Wave, 2021.

LaDyne, Rebekkah. *The Mind-Body Stress Reset: Somatic Practices to Reduce Overwhelm and Increase Well-Being.* Oakland: New Harbinger, 2020.

Levine, Peter. *Healing Trauma: A Pioneering Program for Restoring the Wisdom of Your Body.* Boulder, CO: Sounds True, 2008.

Porges, Stephen. *Polyvagal Safety: Attachment, Communication, Self-Regulation.* New York: Norton, 2021.

Self-Trust, Self-Compassion, and Boundaries

Brown, Brené. "The Anatomy of Trust." Super Soul Sessions, November 1, 2015. https://brenebrown.com/videos/anatomy-trust-video/.

———. *Braving the Wilderness: The Quest for True Belonging and the Courage to Stand Alone.* New York: Random House, 2017.

Germer, Christopher K., and Kristin Neff. *Mindful Self-Compassion Workbook: A Proven Way to Accept Yourself, Build Inner Strength, and Thrive.* New York: Guilford, 2018.

Neff, Kristin. *Self-Compassion: How Women Can Harness Kindness to Speak Up, Claim Their Power, and Thrive.* New York: Harper Wave, 2021.

———. *Self-Compassion: The Proven Power of Being Kind to Yourself.* New York: Morrow, 2011.

Tawwab, Nedra Glover. *Set Boundaries, Find Peace: A Guide to Reclaiming Yourself.* New York: TarcherPerigee, 2021.

Grieving the Life You Once Had

Cain, Susan. *Bittersweet: How Sorrow and Longing Make Us Whole.* New York: Crown, 2022.

Cortman, Chris, and Joseph Walden. *Keep Pain in the Past: Getting Over Trauma, Grief and the Worst That's Ever Happened to You.* Coral Gables, FL: Mango, 2018.

Devine, Megan. *It's OK That You're Not OK.* Boulder, CO: Sounds True, 2017.

O'Connor, Mary-Frances. *The Grieving Brain: The Surprising Science of How We Learn from Love and Loss*. New York: HarperOne, 2022.

Olivera, Lisa. *Already Enough: A Path to Self-Acceptance*. New York: Simon & Schuster, 2022.

Rohr, Richard. *Breathing under Water: Spirituality and the Twelve Steps*. Cincinnati: Franciscan Media, 2011.

Accessing a Robust Spectrum of Emotions

Bradshaw, John. *Homecoming: Reclaiming and Championing Your Inner Child*. New York: Bantam Books, 1990.

Chemaly, Soraya L. *Rage Becomes Her: The Power of Women's Anger*. New York: Atria Books, 2018.

Holmes, Tom, with Lauri Holmes. *Parts Work: An Illustrated Guide to Your Inner Life*. Kalamazoo, MI: Winged Heart, 2007.

Selvam, Raja. *The Practice of Embodying Emotions: A Guide for Improving Cognitive, Emotional, and Behavioral Outcomes*. Berkeley: North Atlantic Books, 2022.

Truman, Karol K. *Feelings Buried Alive Never Die*. Phoenix: Olympus, 1991.

Reclaiming Sexuality and Pleasure

Anderson, Dianna E. *Damaged Goods: New Perspectives on Christian Purity*. New York: Jericho Books, 2015.

Bolz-Weber, Nadia. *Shameless: A Sexual Reformation*. New York: Convergent, 2019.

brown, adrienne maree. *Pleasure Activism: The Politics of Feeling Good*. Chino, CA: AK Press, 2019.

Cooper, Brittney C. *Eloquent Rage: A Black Feminist Discovers Her Superpower*. New York: St. Martin's Press, 2018.

Levine, Peter. *Sexual Healing: Transforming the Sacred Wound*. Boulder, CO: Sounds True, 2003. Audiobook, 2 hrs., 3 min.

Moultrie, Monique Nicole. *Passionate and Pious: Religious Media and Black Women's Sexuality*. Durham, NC: Duke University Press, 2017.

Nagoski, Emily. *Come as You Are: The Surprising New Science That Will Transform Your Sex Life*. New York: Simon & Schuster, 2015.

Richmond, Holly. *Reclaiming Pleasure: A Sex Positive Guide for Moving Past Sexual Trauma and Living a Passionate Life*. Oakland: New Harbinger, 2021.

Roberts, Matthias. *Beyond Shame: Creating a Healthy Sex Life on Your Own Terms*. Minneapolis: Fortress, 2020.

Sellers, Tina Schermer. *Sex, God and the Conservative Church: Erasing Shame from Sexual Intimacy*. New York: Routledge, 2017.

Smith, Erica. The Purity Culture Dropout Program, webinar series, https://www.ericasmitheac.com/webinars-books.

Establishing Healthy Connection and Relationships

Brown, Brené. "The Anatomy of Trust." SuperSoul Sessions, November 1, 2015. https://brenebrown.com/videos/anatomy-trust-video/.

Earnshaw, Elizabeth. *I Want This to Work: An Inclusive Guide to Navigating the Most Difficult Relationship Issues We Face in the Modern Age*. Boulder, CO: Sounds True, 2021.

Gibson, Lindsay. *Adult Children of Emotionally Immature Parents: How to Heal from Distant, Rejecting, or Self-Involved Parents*. Oakland: New Harbinger, 2015.

Heller, Diane Poole. *The Power of Attachment: How to Create Deep and Lasting Intimate Relationships*. Boulder, CO: Sounds True, 2019.

Kim, John, and Vanessa Bennett. *It's Not Me, It's You: Break the Blame Cycle. Relationship Better*. New York: HarperOne, 2022.

Lue, Natalie. *Mr. Unavailable and the Fallback Girl*. Self-published, CreateSpace, 2011.

Pharaon, Vienna. *The Origins of You: How Breaking Family Patterns Can Liberate the Way We Live and Love*. New York: Putnam, 2023.

Richo, David. *How to Be an Adult: A Handbook on Psychological and Spiritual Integration*. New York: Paulist Press, 1991.

Tatkin, Stan. *Wired for Love: How Understanding Your Partner's Brain and Attachment Style Can Help You Defuse Conflict and Build a Secure Relationship*. Oakland: New Harbinger, 2011.

———. *Your Brain on Love: The Neurobiology of Healthy Relationships*. Boulder, CO: Sounds True, 2013. Audiobook, 5 hrs. 50 min.

Webster, Bethany. *Discovering the Inner Mother: A Guide to Healing the Mother Wound and Claiming Your Personal Power*. New York: William Morrow, 2021.

Integrating the Living Legacy of Trauma

Atlas, Galit. *Emotional Inheritance: A Therapist, Her Patients, and the Legacy of Trauma*. New York: Little, Brown Spark, 2022.

Bryant, Thema. *Homecoming: Overcome Fear and Trauma to Reclaim Your Whole, Authentic Self*. New York: TarcherPerigee, 2022.

Clayton, Ingrid. *Believing Me: Healing from Narcissistic Abuse and Complex Trauma*. Self-published, My Own Voice Publishing, 2022.

Fisher, Janina. *Healing the Fragmented Selves of the Trauma Survivor: Overcoming Internal Self-Alienation*. New York: Routledge, 2017.

———. *Transforming the Living Legacy of Trauma: A Workbook for Survivors and Therapists*. Eau Claire, WI: PESI, 2021.

Foo, Stephanie. *What My Bones Know: A Memoir of Healing from Complex Trauma*. New York: Ballantine Books, 2022.

Frank, Britt. *The Science of Stuck: Breaking through Inertia to Find Your Path Forward*. New York: TarcherPerigee, 2022.

Nagoski, Emily, and Amelia Nagoski. *Burnout: The Secret to Unlocking the Stress Cycle*. New York: Ballantine Books, 2019.

Nakazawa, Donna Jackson. *Childhood Disrupted: How Your Biography Becomes Your Biology, and How You Can Heal*. New York: Atria, 2016.

Rothschild, Babette. *The Body Remembers*. Vol. 2 of *Revolutionizing Trauma Treatment*. New York: Norton, 2017.

Schwartz, Arielle. *The Complex PTSD Workbook: A Mind-Body Approach to Regaining Emotional Control and Becoming Whole*. Berkeley: Althea, 2016.

Schwartz, Richard. *No Bad Parts: Healing Trauma and Restoring Wholeness with the Internal Family Systems Model*. Boulder, CO: Sounds True, 2021.

———. *You Are the One You've Been Waiting For: Applying Internal Family Systems to Intimate Relationships*. Boulder, CO: Sounds True, 2023.

Professional Trauma Support

Center for Trauma Resolution and Recovery: www.traumaresolution
andrecovery.com

Reclamation Collective: www.reclamationcollective.com

Religious Trauma Institute: www.religioustraumainstitute.com

For more resources on finding professional support near you, visit
the Center for Trauma Resolution and Recovery's resource page:
www.traumaresolutionandrecovery.com/recommended-resources

LAURA E. ANDERSON, PhD, LMFT, is a licensed psychotherapist in Nashville, Tennessee, with specialties in domestic violence, sexualized violence, and religious trauma. She is the co-founder of the Religious Trauma Institute, which provides clinical training, supervision, consultation, and support to therapists, coaches, advocates, and others in the helping professions who are working with individuals experiencing religious trauma and adverse religious experiences. Laura is also the founder of the Center for Trauma Resolution and Recovery, an online coaching practice whose practitioners are trauma informed and trained to work with all types of trauma but specialize in and are passionate about working with religious trauma. Learn more at www.drlauraeanderson.com.